THE EMERGING CHRISTIAN MINORITY

The Pro Ecclesia Series

Books in The Pro Ecclesia Series are "for the church." The series is sponsored by the Center for Catholic and Evangelical Theology, founded by Carl Braaten and Robert Jenson in 1991. The series seeks to nourish the church's faithfulness to the gospel of Jesus Christ through a theology that is self-critically committed to the biblical, dogmatic, liturgical, and ethical traditions that form the foundation for a fruitful ecumenical theology. The series reflects a commitment to the classical tradition of the church as providing the resources critically needed by the various churches as they face modern and post-modern challenges. The series will include books by individuals as well as collections of essays by individuals and groups. The Editorial Board will be drawn from various Christian traditions.

The Emerging
Christian Minority

edited by

Victor Lee Austin &
Joel C. Daniels

CASCADE *Books* · Eugene, Oregon

THE EMERGING CHRISTIAN MINORITY

Pro Ecclesia Series 8

Cascade Books
An Imprint of Wipf and Stock Publishers
199 W. 8th Ave., Suite 3
Eugene, OR 97401

www.wipfandstock.com

PAPERBACK ISBN: 978-1-5326-3102-3
HARDCOVER ISBN: 978-1-5326-3104-7
EBOOK ISBN: 978-1-5326-3103-0

Cataloguing-in-Publication data:

Names: Austin, Victor Lee, editor. | Daniels, Joel C., editor.

Title: The emerging Christian minority / edited by Victor Lee Austin and Joel C. Daniels.

Description: Eugene, OR : Cascade Books, 2019 | Pro Ecclesia Series 8 | Includes bibliographical references and index.

Identifiers: ISBN 978-1-5326-3102-3 (paperback) | ISBN 978-1-5326-3104-7 (hardcover) | ISBN 978-1-5326-3103-0 (ebook)

Subjects: LCSH: Secularization (Theology). | Christianity—21st century. | Christianity and other religions. | Civilization, Western.

Classification: BR481 .E53 2019 (print) | BR481 .E53 (ebook)

Manufactured in the USA.   FEBRUARY 5, 2019

Chapter 5 originally appeared in Joseph Small, *Flawed Church, Faithful God* (Grand Rapids, MI: Eerdmans, 2018). Reprinted by permission of the publisher; all rights reserved.

Table of Contents

List of Contributors · vii

Preface · ix
VICTOR LEE AUSTIN AND JOEL C. DANIELS

1. Is It Good to Be Persecuted? · 1
   WILLIAM T. CAVANAUGH

2. St. Augustine on the Church as Sacrifice, Then and Now · 20
   PAIGE E. HOCHSCHILD

3. To Be a Minority · 43
   DAVID NOVAK

4. A Tree Planted by Streams of Water: Scriptural Lessons on Hope · 62
   KATHRYN SCHIFFERDECKER

5. Professing the Faith in "A Secular Age" · 82
   JOSEPH D. SMALL

6. Orthodoxy in America: A Minority That Came of Age · 99
   ANTON C. VRAME

List of contributors

Victor Lee Austin, the Program Director of the Center for Catholic and Evangelical Theology, is Theologian-in-residence of the Episcopal Diocese of Dallas and Church of the Incarnation, Dallas. His publications include *Up with Authority: Why We Need Authority to Flourish as Human Beings* (Bloomsbury, 2010), *Christian Ethics: A Guide for the Perplexed* (Bloomsbury, 2012), and, most recently, *Losing Susan: Brain Disease, the Priest's Wife, and the God Who Gives and Takes Away* (Brazos, 2016).

William T. Cavanaugh is Director of the Center for World Catholicism and Intercultural Theology and Professor of Catholic Studies at DePaul University. He is the author of seven books, including *The Myth of Religious Violence: Secular Ideology and the Roots of Modern Conflict* (Oxford University Press, 2009) and *Field Hospital: The Church's Engagement with a Wounded World* (Eerdmans, 2016). He co-edits the journal *Modern Theology*. He has lectured on six continents, and his writings have been published in twelve languages.

Joel C. Daniels is Rector of the Nevil Memorial Church of Saint George in Ardmore, Pennsylvania, and postdoctoral fellow at the Center for Mind and Culture. His monograph, *Theology, Tragedy, and Suffering in Nature: Toward a Realist Doctrine of Creation*, was published by Peter Lang in 2016 as part of the Studies in Episcopal and Anglican Theology series. He is Assistant Editor of the journal *Religion, Brain & Behavior*, adjunct faculty at Fordham University and the General Theological Seminary, and serves on the board of directors of the Society of Scholar-Priests.

Paige E. Hochschild is on the theology faculty of Mount St. Mary's University, in Emmitsburg, Maryland. Her most recent publication is *Memory in Augustine's Theological Anthropology* (Oxford University Press, 2012).

David Novak is the Richard and Dorothy Shiff Chair of Jewish Studies at the University of Toronto. He is the author of *Jewish Justice: The Contested Limits of Nature, Law, and Covenant* (Baylor University Press, 2017), *The Sanctity of Human Life* (Georgetown University Press, 2009), and *Talking with Christians: Musings of a Jewish Theologian* (Eerdmans, 2005). His book, *Covenantal Rights: A Study in Jewish Political Theory* (Princeton University Press, 2000), won the annual award of the American Academy of Religion for "best book in constructive religious thought."

Kathryn Schifferdecker is Associate Professor of Old Testament at Luther Seminary, St. Paul, Minnesota. She is the author of *Out of the Whirlwind: Creation Theology in the Book of Job* (Harvard University Press, 2008). She is a regular contributor to Workingpreacher.org and *Word & World*.

Joseph D. Small served as director of the Presbyterian Church (USA.) Office of Theology and Worship from 1989–2011. He is currently adjunct faculty at the University of Dubuque Theological Seminary, the Reformed Institute of Metropolitan Washington, and church relations consultant to the Presbyterian Foundation. He is the author of, among other books, *To Be Reformed: Living the Tradition* (Witherspoon Press, 2010) and *Let Us Reason Together: Christians and Jews in Conversation* (Witherspoon Press, 2010). His *festschrift, Theology in Service of the Church: Essays in Honor of Joseph D. Small 3rd*, was published in 2008 (Geneva Press).

Anton C. Vrame is Director of the Department of Religious Education of the Greek Orthodox Archdiocese of America. He is also Adjunct Associate Professor of Religious Education at Holy Cross Greek Orthodox School of Theology. He has focused much of his research on the sociology of the Orthodox Christian churches in the United States, which has led him to examine the history of Orthodoxy in America. He is a member of the Convening Table on Theological Dialogue on Matters of Faith and Order (the Faith and Order Commission) of the National Council of Churches, and served for five years as the Chair of Faith and Order. He is a priest of the Greek Orthodox Archdiocese of America.

Preface

Victor Lee Austin and Joel C. Daniels

Ever since the Edict of Milan in AD 313, the Christian church has enjoyed a special relationship with civic authorities in Western Europe. The reign of Christendom—a catch-all term for the social, political, and cultural privileges enjoyed by the Christian church—was an integral component in the development of Europe from the Middle Ages onward. While its vestiges may remain, Christendom finds itself losing ground rapidly. Part of this retreat is due to the growing proportion of non-Christian religions in the West, but most of it has to do with increased secularization and a general turn away from religion altogether. According to the Pew Research Forum, the primary driver in decreasing rates of service attendance and beliefs in the United States is the rise of the "nones": persons who claim no religious affiliation at all, particularly those born after 1980.[1] As of 2015, the religiously unaffiliated accounted for 23 percent of all American adults; the group accounted for 16 percent in 2007.

What does this changing landscape mean for existing Christian communities? Are there biblical or historical precedents for this situation? What should we expect in the future? These were the issues taken up by the speakers at the 2016 conference, "The Emerging Christian Minority," sponsored by the Center for Catholic and Evangelical Theology. Each author here addresses the topic from a different perspective. Given the historical relationship between persecution and church vitality, William Cavanaugh asks, "Is it good to be persecuted?" Paige E. Hochschild discusses Augustine's

1. http://www.pewforum.org/2015/11/03/u-s-public-becoming-less-religious/.

reflections on the church as sacrifice. David Novak, a rabbi, makes an in-
terfaith contribution by discussing the Jewish experience of minority status
in the West. Kathryn Schifferdecker finds hope for the future in the words
of Scripture, specifically in the book of Job. Joseph Small looks to the early
church and the church in the global south to reflect on the place of the
gospel in an age of secularization. Finally, Anthony Vrame examines the
archives of the Greek Orthodox Archdiocese of America to tell the story of
that communion's growth in a foreign land: the United States.

There is no doubt that the religious landscape in the United States
will continue to shift, with some consequences that cannot be predicted. As
these writers show, however, these changes provide the church with opportunities as well as challenges. We hope that these collected reflections can
serve as an inspiration to Christian communities, who seem to be emerging
into a minority status, to increase their faith in the one who promised to be
with us always, even to the end of the age.

Victor Lee Austin, Episcopal Diocese of Dallas
Joel C. Daniels, Nevil Memorial Church
of St. George and Center for Mind and Culture

1

Is It Good to Be Persecuted?

William T. Cavanaugh

Is IT GOOD TO be persecuted? No, it's not. It is not good to be persecuted. It is bad to be persecuted.

I am tempted to stop there, but the editors of this volume who gave me the title for my paper would probably not be pleased. They clearly had more in mind than the simple question of whether or not being on the receiving end of persecution is a good thing. No sane person would say that being tortured and executed for one's faith is positive. But one could make the argument that the church is stronger and better under persecution. The intensity and devotion of Polish and Irish Catholicism in the twentieth century is often attributed to the persecution of the church under the Communists and the British. It might not be a coincidence that Catholic practice in Ireland has taken a steep dive since the peace accord was signed on Good Friday in 1998. Likewise, the Catholic Church in Chile seems to have lost much of its sense of purpose now that it doesn't have General Pinochet to kick it around anymore.

Even if one buys that argument on a purely sociological basis, however, there are few who would demand the return of human rights abuses so that the church could feel needed again. But there could be a sense, as Candida Moss puts it, that "In Christian terms, if you're being persecuted, you must be doing something right."[1] Persecution, in these terms, is not something to be desired, either for its own sake or for some end such as strengthening the church, but when found it is an indicator that Christians

1. Candida Moss, *The Myth of Persecution: How Early Christians Invented a Story of Martyrdom* (New York: HarperOne, 2013), 250.

have taken the high moral ground. The fact of being persecuted could then be worn as a badge of honor. Claiming to be persecuted could be used as evidence of the rightness of one's cause, and therefore also as evidence of the depravity of one's opponents. Claiming to be a victim of persecution could have the effect of galvanizing the church around a righteous cause, indeed the cause of Jesus Christ and the martyrs who also suffered persecution for righteousness's sake. Persecution could also be a rallying point around which to draw outsiders to sympathize with the church's plight.

There is a sense among many Christians today that Christians are not only rapidly becoming a minority in American society, but are becoming a persecuted minority. The campaign for religious liberty that the Catholic bishops and others have put forward is in many ways a response to this sense that the church is vulnerable to officially sanctioned interference and even persecution for sticking to its principles in a rapidly changing society. In the midst of the 2012 election campaign, Francis Cardinal George of Chicago repeated in print his famous off-the-cuff remark that he "expected to die in bed, my successor will die in prison, and his successor will die a martyr in the public square." In the same column he wrote, "Secularism is communism's better-scrubbed bedfellow," and denounced "the anti-religious sentiment, much of it explicitly anti-Catholic, that has been growing in this country for several decades."[2]

The rhetoric of Cardinal George and others has evoked a reaction not only among secularists but among some Christians who have criticized such language for its polarizing effects on our discourse. Candida Moss, formerly of Notre Dame and now professor of theology at the University of Birmingham in the United Kingdom, has gone further, and located a kind of persecution complex endemic to Christianity which she sees as responsible for coarsening our current political debates. Moss's book *The Myth of Persecution* (2013) is a full-frontal attack on the way Christians have narrated the history of early Christian martyrdom. According to Moss, the tales of relentless Roman persecution of Christians are largely fabrications of the postmartyrdom period meant to lend legitimacy to orthodox

2. Francis Cardinal George, OMI, "The Wrong Side of History," para. 4, *Catholic New World*, October 21–November 3, 2012, https://www.chicagocatholic.com/cardinal-george/-/article/2012/10/21/the-wrong-side-of-history. Cardinal George also pointed out that his famous quote about martyrdom in fact continued with a more hopeful speculation about the martyred bishop's successor: "His successor will pick up the shards of a ruined society and slowly help rebuild civilization, as the Church has done so often in human history."

Christian power. Although Moss is an academic, her book was published by a popular press, HarperOne, and it is aimed at and has found a general audience. The book is not just about the past, but about how the rhetoric of persecution has poisoned political and cultural debates in the present by allowing Christians to proclaim victim status and demonize opponents.

In this chapter, I will examine the rhetoric of persecution among Christians from two opposing points of view, that of Moss and that of the U. S. Catholic Bishops' campaign for religious liberty. I will argue that both are seriously flawed, and for the same reason: neither can countenance the idea that there could be a fundamental tension between being an American and being a Christian. I will look at Moss's book and the Bishops' campaign in turn, and then at the end point toward a Christian theology of persecution.

Subsumed under the State

Although the target of Moss's book is Christian rhetoric about persecution in the US, her book begins with a description of the 2011 bombing of a Coptic church in Egypt. In the aftermath, the dead were referred to by some as "martyrs." Christian protestors in response targeted Muslim institutions. According to Moss, there is a direct causal link between these two facts: naming the victims as martyrs theologized the violence and enhanced the perception among Christians that they are engaged in a perpetual conflict of good versus evil: Christianity against the world. "Ironically, it is the belief that Christians are persecuted that empowered the protestors to attack others."[3]

But clearly Christians *are* persecuted in Egypt, though we can agree that retaliatory violence is not good. Moss, however, does not want us to make such distinctions; she uses the Egypt example as evidence that claiming to be persecuted should be avoided because it leads to violence. "The rhetoric of persecution legitimates and condones retributive violence,"[4] even, apparently, in places where the fact of persecution can hardly be denied. Moss then switches from Egypt to the United States, and argues that Christians' claims of being persecuted are spurious, and that such claims lead to an unhealthy polarization of American public discourse. Such claims are, furthermore, not just a contemporary aberration, but are hardwired into Christian rhetoric by a false reading of Christian history

3. Moss, *Myth of Persecution,* 3.
4. Ibid., 3.

invented largely in the fourth century. That reading of history—of which Eusebius is the main culprit—presents the early church as a church of martyrs heroically bearing up under relentless Roman persecution, and paints the rest of Christian history as the continuation of this brave resistance to the forces of evil. The church even came to see martyrdom in a positive light;[5] according to Moss, in the early church, "the majority started to see the suffering of the innocent as a good thing."[6] This martyr complex continues to poison our public discourse:

> The view that the history of Christianity is a history of unrelenting persecution persists in modern religious and political debate about what it means to be a Christian. It creates a world in which Christians are under attack; it endorses political warfare rather than encouraging political discourse; and it legitimizes seeing those who disagree with us as our enemies.[7]

Moss's prime example of this type of rhetoric is a 2012 sermon given by Daniel Jenky, Catholic bishop of Peoria, Illinois, calling for heroic opposition to the Health and Human Services mandate requiring all employers—including Catholic institutions—to facilitate insurance coverage for contraception for their employees. Jenky infamously compared the Obama administration to those of Hitler and Stalin, and vowed that the church would resist persecution, as it always had. "For 2,000 years," the bishop said, "the enemies of Christ have certainly tried their best."[8] Jenky cited the "terrible persecution" of the church under the Roman Empire, barbarian invasions, Nazi and Communist rule, the "hatred of Hollywood," and other attacks on Christianity, but declared that the church had survived them all, and would continue to do so. Persecution is nothing new; the devil "will always hate us,"[9] according to Jenky.

For Moss, Jenky's sermon is one example of a broader idea that is "hardwired into Christian history"[10]: "Christians have claimed that from the dawn of Christianity right up to the present day they have faced continual

---

5. "The way the early Christians tell it, martyrdom was a necessary part of Christian existence and fostered the survival of Christianity" (ibid., 7).

6. Ibid., 5.

7. Ibid., 21.

8. Bishop Daniel R. Jenky, quoted in Moss, *Myth of Persecution,* 10.

9. Ibid., 10.

10. Ibid., 128.

and relentless opposition and persecution."[11] Moss is so determined to root out this pernicious view of Christian history that she is prepared to burn down the entire edifice of Christian martyrology and a good deal of Christian historiography with it. She responds to the idea that Christians have virtually always been persecuted with the notion that Christians have virtually never been persecuted. She begins by questioning the uniqueness of Christian martyrdom, pointing out that other people died for their convictions before Christianity; they were martyrs, though they didn't use the term.[12] Moss then takes an extremely jaundiced view of the scriptural accounts of Jesus' suffering and of the early acts of the martyrs. None of them can be trusted to be historically accurate; they are full of borrowings from pagan literature and of outright fabrications. Luke, for example, has taken Mark's weak, anxiety-ridden Jesus at his passion and made him into Socrates, stoically accepting death.[13] Moss omits Luke's mention of angels and sweating blood (Luke 22:43–44), claiming in an endnote that those verses must have been later additions to Luke's text.[14]

The early Christian martyr accounts fare even worse. According to Moss, there are only six martyrdom stories that preserve anything of historical truth, and even those stories have been tampered with by later Christians to further their own theological agendas.[15] By the time Moss gets done picking apart *The Martyrdom of Polycarp*—the earliest surviving martyrdom account and one of the six reliable ones—there is nothing left but the bare fact that a guy named Polycarp was killed:

> Polycarp was almost certainly executed by the Romans, but we really don't know anything about the circumstances of his arrest, trial, and death. This makes it impossible to know the reason he was executed or the principles he died for. If all we can know is the fact of his execution, then we have to face the possibility that the martyr we admire is the invention of the author.[16]

11. Ibid., 125.

12. Ibid., 28–29.

13. Ibid., 58–61.

14. Ibid., 267n5. The verses from Luke read "Then an angel from heaven appeared to him and gave him strength. In his anguish he prayed more earnestly, and his sweat became like great drops of blood falling down on the ground" (Luke 22:43–44, NRSV).

15. Ibid., 16–17.

16. Ibid., 104.

Moss concludes that "the earliest martyrdom account…is a pious fraud."[17] The other five supposedly reliable accounts fare no better. Any account that presents the Christian martyrs in a positive light is treated with extreme skepticism. Those that present the Christian martyrs in a negative light, on the other hand, are taken at face value, like Tertullian's fantastical tale about an incident in which "in Asia Minor in the second century thousands of Christians banged on the door of the Roman proconsul's house and demanded to be executed as Christians."[18] Did the thousands take turns knocking, or was it a really big door? How did Tertullian—and no one else, apparently—come to know about this incident in Asia Minor, given that he never left Africa?

Moss asks no such questions of this account, because suicidal Christians are useful for debunking the idea that Christian martyrs are always good or always died as a result of persecution. In addition to Tertullian's tale, Moss cites the story of Agathonike who threw herself on the flames at another Christian's martyrdom. Moss raises no questions about the historicity of this text. Likewise, all Moss's doubts about the *Acts of Ptolemy and Lucius*—one of the six that she subjects to withering criticism in chapter 3—seem to vanish in chapter 6, when she cites this text for its reference to an unnamed man who came forward of his own accord and was subsequently killed.[19]

Some early Christian martyrs, claims Moss, were not only suicidal, but homicidal. Here she can muster but two examples, neither of which are very convincing. One is from a Coptic text—again, no questions asked—in which a young Christian grabs a sword in the courtroom and is promptly killed by Roman soldiers. The other is of the Circumcellions, a fringe sect of the Donatists who killed other Christians and tried to provoke their own deaths in order to achieve "martyrdom."[20] Not only were the Circumcellions a sect of a sect, but they came after the age of martyrs, and, as Moss admits in an endnote, we know virtually nothing about them except from the writings of their opponents.[21]

17. Ibid., 104.

18. Ibid., 192.

19. Ibid., 191–93. Moss's critique of the *Acts of Ptolemy and Lucius* is in chapter 3, pages 105–9. Moss concludes of the text, written by Justin Martyr, "We'll never know for certain what Lucius said or even if there was a Lucius at all. All we have is a literary mouthpiece for Justin's own views" (ibid., 109).

20. Ibid., 196–97.

21. Ibid., 286n3.

Unable to come up with a single pre-Constantine example of actual violence committed by Christian martyrs, Moss turns to the martyrs' "rhetorical violence." According to Moss, "In some circumstances their confessions are acts of violence"[22] because they cast their deaths in terms of triumph over the devil,[23] and because they imply that their judges and executioners will face judgment after they die.[24] Moss finds such high-stakes language in the face of death understandable, but troubling nonetheless. "It's easy to miss, but in referring to 'the devil's' or 'Satan's' efforts to overwhelm the Christians, we forget that there are human actors in these events. Judges, torturers, and 'the crowd' are dehumanized."[25] Moss is right to be wary of dehumanizing one's enemies, but sympathizing with the torturer who is suffering from the violent rhetoric of the person he is torturing seems a little perverse. The act of torturing someone, not the rhetoric, is what dehumanizes the torturer. Moss rightly says that we should be concerned about what happens when this rhetoric of good and evil is translated into situations where Christians are not the underdogs.[26] She reaches forward seven centuries to the Crusades to make this point. It seems to me, however, that we can distinguish between martyrdom and the Crusades. Sometimes Christians really are tortured and killed—today's world is full of such cases—and that is evil. Moss is clearly uncomfortable with any language about Satan, but like it or not, the devil is recognized in Christian tradition as more than a rhetorical device. Moss is right that we need to exercise caution in claiming that someone is in the grip of Satan, but such language does not necessarily dehumanize; it can be a way of saying "they know not what they do."

At the heart of the matter here is Moss's reluctance to allow the possibility that Christians really could be at odds with what the Gospel of John calls "the world," or what we might call the status quo. Moss makes the case that not only were persecutions of Christians in the Roman Empire

22. Ibid., 204.

23. Moss gives the following example from the *Martyrs of Lyons*, referring to Sanctus's body after torture: "But his body bore witness to his sufferings, being all one bruise and all one wound, stretched and distorted out of any recognizably human shape; but Christ suffering in him achieved great glory, overwhelming the Adversary, and showing as an example to all the others that nothing is to be feared where the Father's love is, nothing painful where we find Christ's glory" (ibid., 197–98).

24. Ibid., 204–7.

25. Ibid., 199.

26. Ibid., 200.

sporadic and localized—a fact on which all histories of the early church agree—but that they don't really qualify as persecutions at all. The crucial distinction is between persecution and prosecution. According to Moss, "A persecutor targets representatives of a specific group for undeserved punishment merely because of their participation in that group. An individual is prosecuted because that person has broken a law."[27] Moss acknowledges that "It is simply anachronistic to divide ancient motivations into the religious and the political."[28] She uses this point to admonish the reader not to impose our modern ideas of religious freedom on the Romans.[29] When it suits her purposes, however, she embraces the "simply anachronistic" religion/politics distinction to claim that Roman treatment of Christians was politically, not religiously, motivated, and therefore it qualified as prosecution, not persecution. Thus "Even the so-called Decian persecution in 250 CE was about political uniformity, not religious persecution."[30] Decius issued a decree that all must either sacrifice to the Roman gods or die. But Moss argues that Decius was not really all that interested in Christians; his real mission was to unify an empire under threat from Goths from without and political rivals from within. "The decree was about social conformity and political loyalty . . . That Christians were caught in the crosshairs of Decius's efforts to secure his empire is deeply unfortunate, but it is not evidence of anti-Christian legislation. This is prosecution, not persecution."[31] Moss treats Valerian the same way. She compares his decree of death for all Christian bishops, priests, deacons, senators, and high-ranking officials to the British law that, until recently, prohibited the monarch from marrying a Roman Catholic. "In the same way, Valerian's suppression of Christianity was not about persecuting Christians in general; it was about preserving the integrity of the Roman government and limiting the influence of what

27. Ibid., 14.

28. Ibid., 174; she makes the same point on page 14 and on page 186. Moss is right about this point, and this point has important consequences that she goes on to ignore. I have argued at length elsewhere that the religion/politics distinction is a modern Western invention and does not apply to the ancient world. We should therefore avoid making claims about the violence of "religion" in the ancient world, as if "religion" were something clearly distinct from "politics." How could it be if Caesar is a god? See chapter 2 of my book *The Myth of Religious Violence: Secular Ideology and the Roots of Modern Conflict* (New York: Oxford University Press, 2009).

29. Moss, *Myth of Persecution,* 174.

30. Ibid., 15.

31. Ibid., 150–51.

was seen as a potentially destructive group."[32] Only Diocletian's persecution really counts as persecution, and to that Moss adds so many qualifiers and mitigating circumstances that she concludes "It was really only after Diocletian's fourth edict in 304, only in select regions in the empire, and presumably only until his retirement in 305 that we find the kind of situation assumed by the myth of Christian persecution."[33]

According to Moss, the idea that Christians were "mercilessly thrown to lions merely for their religious beliefs is a macabre fairy tale."[34] Moss argues that

> if we make the (arguably anachronistic) move of divorcing religion and politics, then the prosecution of early Christians is better understood as politically motivated. If the Roman emperors had a problem with Christians and Christianity, it was because they threatened the stability of the empire and appeared to make divisive political claims. Roman emperors did not take issue with nonthreatening things like baptism or hymns; they had problems with those aspects of Christianity that sounded like treason or revolution.[35]

Those aspects included Christian refusal to serve in the military, which Moss remarks was "almost unheard of before Christians."[36] Likewise, the imperial cult was something that bound the empire together, like the pledge of allegiance, says Moss.[37] To refuse to participate was seen as sedition. Christians also recognized only the authority of God, not the authority of courts or government. When people act this way today, we regard them as "either sinister or vaguely insane. Even modern societies work on the basis of a social contract by which individual beliefs are subsumed under the state."[38] We can hardly blame the Romans for being taken aback.

32. Ibid., 153.

33. Ibid., 161–62.

34. Ibid., 186.

35. Ibid., 174. The parenthetical remark about anachronism is Moss's own. She again makes the anachronistic division of religion and politics when she writes "The idea that a person could not obey both God and emperor was utterly alien and strikingly dangerous. To a Roman judge it sounded like sedition and political—not religious—subversion" (ibid., 178).

36. Ibid., 176.

37. Ibid., 175.

38. Ibid., 177.

Moss adds, "The Romans rarely persecuted Christians, and when they did, they had logical reasons that made sense to any ancient Roman. This was not blind hatred or mindless persecution."[39] This does not make the Romans' actions just, Moss says, but it does make them intelligible. Moss elicits no such sympathy for Eusebius, who in Moss's telling invented the myth of persecution in order to lend the authority of the martyrs to fourth-century struggles against heresy. Here is where the religion/politics distinction does some heavy lifting for Moss. Roman suppression of Christianity was political, and therefore understandable, if regrettable. Moss makes clear that Christians were suppressed as subversives, not as heretics.[40] Once Christians took charge of the empire, however, they began persecuting heretics for merely religious reasons. It is the Christians, not the Romans, who are the true persecutors.

Moss's targets, of course, are not primarily in the past, but in the present. The point of the book is to reject the idea that American Christians today are persecuted and to reject the rhetorical use of persecution in defense of Christian values. Christianity has made persecution a sign of moral righteousness and a sign of the evil in one's opponents. Persecution is, by definition, unjust. It is a sign not just of disagreement, but of irrational hatred. The claim to be persecuted cuts off the possibility of common ground and compromise with those with whom one disagrees.

I agree with Moss that there is a lot of rhetorical excess in our current public debate, and that common ground and civility are desirable goals. The problem with Moss's argument, however, is that she sees opposition between the church and the world as a symptom of pathology in Christianity. The political realm is one in which we ought to be able to sit down and work out our problems reasonably. Christians might disagree with others on occasion, but it is disagreement, not persecution, and Christians should abide by the political process when they lose. In a pluralistic society, Christians should not insist on expressing their Christianity in public; the normal situation is one in which, as Moss says, "individual beliefs are subsumed under the state."[41] There is no confrontation of good and evil, and there should be no fundamental tension between the social order and Christianity. If there is tension, Moss lays it at the feet of a persecution

39. Ibid., 187.

40. Ibid., 186: "When Christians appeared in Roman courtrooms, they were not tried as heretics, blasphemers, or even fools."

41. As quoted above, ibid., 177.

complex within Christianity. How Jesus got himself killed, and why the New Testament sees tension between the church and the world, are subjects to which I will return later. What I want to note now is the seamless fit between being a Christian and being an American that Moss presumes. The same fit, ironically, is found in her opponents.

Not Having to Choose

It is not a coincidence that Moss's book appeared within a year of the US Catholic bishops launching their campaign for religious liberty, which was largely in response to the Obamacare contraception mandate.[42] The bishops' major document on religious liberty, issued in 2012 and entitled "Our First, Most Cherished Liberty," twice uses the language of persecution, and invokes the memory of the martyrs: "Our liturgical calendar celebrates a series of great martyrs who remained faithful in the face of persecution by political power."[43] The document establishes an annual Fortnight for Freedom, bracketed on one side by the feast of two of those martyrs—St. John Fisher and St. Thomas More on June 21—and on the other side by Independence Day, the Fourth of July. The 2016 Fortnight for Freedom was advertised with a quote from *Fides et Ratio*: "The martyrs give voice to what we already feel and they declare what we would like to have the strength to express."[44] The 2016 theme highlighted 14 individual and group "Witnesses to Freedom," most of whom were martyrs, from the early church to the present, with the conspicuous exception of the Little Sisters of the Poor, who were suing the federal government over the Obamacare mandate.[45]

42. I have written before on the US bishops' campaign for religious liberty. See chapter 12 of my book *Field Hospital: The Church's Engagement with a Wounded World* (Grand Rapids: Eerdmans, 2016), and my chapter entitled "Is Catholicism a Religion? Catholicism and Nationalism in America," in Michael Budde, ed., *Beyond the Borders of Baptism: Catholicity, Allegiances, and Lived Identities* (Eugene, OR: Cascade, 2016).

43. US Conference of Catholic Bishops (USCCB), "Our First, Most Cherished Liberty." http://www.usccb.org/issues-and-action/religious-liberty/our-first-most-cherished-liberty.cfm.

44. See the Fortnight for Freedom 2016 page on the USCCB website: http://www.usccb.org/issues-and-action/religious-liberty/fortnight-for-freedom/index.cfm.

45. The list of Witnesses to Freedom is as follows: Little Sisters of the Poor, Saints John Fisher and Thomas More, Coptic Christians, St. John the Baptist, Venerable Henriette Delille, Blessed Oscar Romero, Martyrs of Compiègne, Fr. John Bapst, SJ, Saints Peter and Paul, Saints Felicity and Perpetua, Blessed Miguel Pro, St. Maximilian Kolbe, St. Edith Stein, and St. Kateri Tekakwitha. See http://www.usccb.org/issues-and-action/

The 2016 Fortnight for Freedom also included an American tour of the relics of the martyred Saints Thomas More and John Fisher.

The bishops' campaign is a clear example of what Moss calls the myth of persecution, but the campaign and Moss's book share the idea that Christianity and the social order should fit seamlessly together. The document "Our First, Most Cherished Liberty" begins "We are Catholics. We are Americans. We are proud to be both, grateful for the gift of faith which is ours as Christian disciples, and grateful for the gift of liberty which is ours as American citizens. To be Catholic and American should mean not having to choose one over the other."[46] In a prayer for the protection of religious liberty that was distributed in parishes throughout the country, the bishops likewise exhort the lay people "to be both engaged and articulate in insisting that as Catholics and as Americans we do not have to choose between the two."

The bishops' campaign has been an odd combination of apocalyptic rhetoric about a church under attack and patriotic language emphasizing the fit between the church and America. Archbishop William Lori's opening homily for the 2013 Fortnight for Freedom was entitled "Faith Enriches Public Life." It is filled with grievances about "governmental authority [that] slices and dices our Church" and a broader secularist hostility that would "diminish the influence of religion in helping to shape the character of our country." It ends with a stirring "may God bless these United States of America!"[47]

The bishops' campaign is replete with patriotic rhetoric. The "Religious Liberty at Home" web page shows a figure in Franciscan garb brandishing a large American flag. The website features American flags prominently. The official prayer for the protection of religious liberty prays "in this decisive hour in the history of our nation" that "this great land will always be 'one nation, under God, indivisible, with liberty and justice for all.'"[48] "Our First, Most Cherished Liberty," is filled with patriotic language about "our enlightened republic," "the land of the free, and a beacon of hope for the

religious-liberty/fortnight-for-freedom/index.cfm.

46. USCCB, "Our First, Most Cherished Liberty," para. 1.

47. Archbishop William Lori, Fortnight for Freedom 2013 opening homily. http://www.usccb.org/issues-and-action/religious-liberty/2013-fortnight-for-freedom-opening-homily-archbishop-william-lori.cfm.

48. USCCB, Mary Immaculate Patroness of Our Country Pray for Us," para. 3. http://www.usccb.org/issues-and-action/religious-liberty/conscience-protection/upload/english-immaculate-conception-religious-liberty-prayer.pdf.

world."[49] Perhaps most remarkable is the "Patriotic Rosary" that has been incorporated into Fortnight for Freedom observances in dioceses across the country.[50] Each bead of the rosary represents one of the fifty states, and before each Hail Mary one pleads the blood of Jesus over that state. Patriotic hymns like the Star-Spangled Banner and the Battle Hymn of the Republic are sung between decades, and the mysteries before each decade are excerpts from the writings of George Washington, John Adams, and other fathers of the nation. The devotees of the Patriotic Rosary presumably are not aware that John Adams once wrote contemptuously of Catholics as "The poor wretches fingering their beads, chanting Latin, not a word of which they understood" or that Adams railed in print against the Catholic Church's "direct and formal design on foot, to enslave America."[51] Speaking of slavery, the fifth mystery is by General Robert E. Lee, writing to his soldiers in the midst of the Civil War about the necessity of "beseeching the aid of the God of our forefathers in the defense of our homes and our liberties,"[52] one liberty of which was the freedom to buy and sell other human beings.

In their statement on religious freedom, the bishops do recognize the possibility that Catholics will face unjust laws that they will need to disobey. They also cite Pope Benedict XVI's statement that the laity should exhibit "a strong critical sense vis-à-vis the dominant culture" in America.[53] But the cultural criticism seems to come from a sense that America was a Christian nation until Obama and the secularists came along to mess it up. The Christian view of marriage, for example, was the law until recently. The apocalyptic language about persecution and martyrdom seems to come from a sense of shock that people do not recognize that Catholicism should fit neatly into American society. The bishops' campaign therefore appeals to the American public to appreciate what religion contributes to America,

---

49. USCCB, "Our First, Most Cherished Liberty," paras. 3, 29.

50. A Google search finds the Patriotic Rosary as part of Fortnight for Freedom celebrations in the (arch)dioceses of Baltimore, Dallas, Wichita, Rockville Centre, Fort Wayne-South Bend, Albany, Washington, DC, Orlando, Yankton, Camden, Milwaukee, etc. etc.

51. John Adams, quoted in Steven Waldman, "Was John Adams an Anti-Catholic Bigot?," para. 3. *Beliefnet,* http://www.beliefnet.com/columnists/stevenwaldman/2008/04/was-john-adams-an-anticatholic.html.

52. Robert E. Lee, quoted in "The Patriotic Rosary," 6. http://www.sacredheartmilledgeville.org/Freedom%20Rosary%20and%20Litany.pdf.

53. USCCB, "Our First, Most Cherished Liberty," para. 8.

and what American ideals of freedom of religion contribute to the church. Appeals to freedom of the individual conscience and appeals to patriotism work together. In the modern age, the church and the nation-state have tended to make their peace by assuming that a Christian's religious allegiance belongs to God and her political allegiance belongs to the nation. The religion/politics divide works the same way here as it does for Moss. Freedom of religion is earned by supporting the political order and not making trouble.

In October of 2005, Stephen Kobasa, a teacher with twenty-five years of service in Catholic schools, was fired from Kolbe Cathedral High School in Bridgeport, Connecticut, for refusing to display the American flag in his classroom. Just before he was fired, Kobasa wrote a letter to the bishop of Bridgeport, explaining that to display the flag "would be to act against my conscience as a believing Roman Catholic Christian. My teaching can never take its legitimacy from any symbol except the Cross of Christ. To elevate any national emblem to that level would be for me to ignore the fundamental call of Jesus to compassion without boundaries."[54] Kobasa added that the threat of dismissal being leveled against him "creates the unmistakable impression that national loyalty is being valued over faithful obedience to the Gospel."[55]

The bishop who fired Stephen Kobasa was William Lori, the current Archbishop of Baltimore and the man in charge of the bishops' campaign for religious freedom.

Siding with the Victims

Having said this, let me be clear that I generally support the aims of the bishops' campaign. I signed onto the Evangelicals and Catholics Together statement In Defense of Religious Freedom. I think the bishops are right to be worried about state coercion aimed at forcing Catholic groups and others to violate their own convictions. I do not think that the issues involved are trivial, though I would hope that the bishops focus less exclusively on the HHS mandate. More attention to the plight of Christians and others around the world who are being murdered for their faith does warrant talk

54. Stephen Kobasa, quoted in Matthew Rothschild, "Catholic High School Teacher Forced Out Over Flag," *The Progressive*, April 18, 2005, http://www.commondreams.org/views05/1018-29.htm.

55. Ibid.

of persecution and martyrdom. Within the US, I agree with Moss that such language is often overblown and unhelpful. There are important distinctions to be made among disagreement, discrimination, and persecution. Those distinctions need to be made carefully, on a case-by-case basis.

Where I think both Moss and the bishops go wrong is in assuming that the political system we have in the United States should—in principle, at least—make conflicts between the church and the social order easy to solve. Both assume that the principle of religious liberty provides a procedural path toward a comfortable fit between Christianity and American society. The truth, however, is that there are deeper disagreements about the nature of the human good that will not be solved procedurally. Liberal democracy might be the best that we can do right now, and we should appreciate its benefits, but it is not the kingdom of God. On its earthly pilgrimage, the people of God will always find itself in tension with the earthly city. We should expect, if not persecution, at least opposition if we are living out the gospel in its fullness.

To say this, however, is not to say that it is good to be persecuted, or, in Moss's words, "to see the suffering of the innocent as a good thing."[56] Moss's argument is not simply with some present-day bishops, but with what she considers the dominant way of reading Christian history and the meaning of Christ's death. According to Moss, for the early Christians, "The fact that the Son of God willingly embraced death for the salvation of others necessarily meant that death for God must be good—otherwise why would he have done it?"[57] Moss asks, "How is it that people can see violence and death as something good and holy?"[58] According to Moss, using Jesus' death as an example to be followed is not something read into the text by overeager followers: "Jesus actually *tells* his followers that they should expect to find themselves arrested."[59]

Moss's narration of Christian readings of atonement seems to assume the hegemony of a rather crude penal substitution theory that valorizes suffering in itself. Penal substitution theories have been rightly criticized by feminist scholars as authorizing a kind of masochism that disproportionately licenses the suffering of women; the key to the imitation of Christ is the embrace of suffering and death as a good, an attitude which lends itself

56. Moss, *Myth of Persecution*, 5.

57. Ibid., 5.

58. Ibid., 4.

59. Ibid., 5.

to the patient endurance of domestic abuse.[60] Other critics have pointed to the way in which penal substitution theories can stoke a vengeful attitude among Christians. Suffering is seen as a good because, as Denny Weaver puts it, "pain balances pain";[61] God needs someone to suffer for the sins of humans. Since God believes in retributive justice, Christians support the death penalty and other ways of balancing suffering with suffering. Such criticisms are rightly directed against penal substitution theories of atonement or any other atonement theories that imply that God requires and valorizes suffering. Moss, however, seems to assume that such theories characterize Christianity *tout court*. She does not regard penal theories of atonement as medieval or early-modern detours, but considers them embedded in the New Testament texts themselves. Moss does not consider the possibility that there are—and always have been—other ways of reading the significance of Jesus' passion and death.

Moss does not seem willing or able to distinguish between saying that opposition and suffering should be expected and saying that opposition and suffering are good. What is needed is a reading of the gospels and a theology of the cross which is capable of making that distinction. In what remains of this chapter, I want to point toward such a reading and theology, though I can't develop it fully. It seems to me that any reasonably attentive reading of the gospels will show that the inbreaking of the kingdom of God can expect to meet with opposition from anti-kingdom forces. In Mark, Jesus' declaration that the kingdom is "at hand" (1:15) is followed by dramatic confrontations with demons, diseases, storms, and the social order maintained by the Romans and the Pharisees. The coming of the Messiah is presented as the climax of history in which the final victory over the forces of evil will be won. But precisely because Jesus is not the warrior Messiah people—including his own disciples—expected, the victory of the kingdom over the anti-kingdom would not be won by inflicting suffering on others. Jesus predicts his own suffering and that of his followers, to the disciples' repeated incomprehension (e.g., 9:30–32). Suffering and persecution is to be expected; faithfulness despite opposition is certainly lauded, but there is no indication that it is good to be persecuted. Jesus—in Mark anyway, as Moss herself notes—does not regard his own death as a badge of honor, but

60. See, for example, Joanne Carlson Brown and Rebecca Parker, "For God So Loved the World?," in Joanne Carlson Brown and Carole R. Bohn, eds., *Christianity, Patriarchy, and Abuse: A Feminist Critique* (New York: Pilgrim, 1989), and Darby Kathleen Ray, *Deceiving the Devil: Atonement, Abuse, and Ransom* (Cleveland: Pilgrim, 1998).

61. J. Denny Weaver, *The Nonviolent God* (Grand Rapids, MI: Eerdmans, 2013), 208.

anticipates it with dread, and indeed asks the Father to take this cup away from him (14:36).

In the worldview presumed by the gospels, to follow Jesus means that you will likely encounter opposition, but you will be on the right side of history. As René Girard interprets it, to be on the right side of history is to side with the victims of this world. Girard's famous theory of violence sees the origin of violence in mimetic rivalries within every society. In order to keep societies from descending into chaos, order is maintained by uniting against common scapegoats, usually chosen from the margins: Jews, blacks, communists, immigrants, and so on. In archaic religion, myth and ritual sacrifice of victims perpetuates such scapegoating and thereby maintains social order. Christianity, however, overturns this social order by declaring that the victim is innocent, and identifying the victim with God in Jesus Christ. Girard considers Christianity to be the unique and earthshaking revelation that the victim is innocent, and that the violent basis on which social order is maintained is a lie.[62] Christianity not only does away with pagan sacrifice, but exposes the scapegoating mechanism that continues to work in supposedly secular social orders through war, the criminal justice system, and other mechanisms.[63]

One thinks here of Martin Luther King Jr.'s letter from the Birmingham jail. He commends the "Negro sit-inners and demonstrators of Birmingham" for "their willingness to suffer,"[64] not because suffering in itself is a good or is God's will, but because their suffering reveals the disorder of what passes for social order in the segregated South. Their suffering is an evil which only becomes necessary in order to reveal the truth of a greater evil, that of segregation and discrimination which goes by the name of "law and order." The suffering of the demonstrators is not generative, but revelatory. As King writes, "we who engage in nonviolent direct action are not the creators of tension. We merely bring to the surface the hidden tension which is already alive. We bring it out in the open where it can be seen and dealt with."[65] Willingness to suffer under these circumstances exposes the

62. Perhaps the most accessible single-volume statement of Girard's theory is found in René Girard, *I See Satan Fall Like Lightning,* trans. James G. Williams (Maryknoll, NY: Orbis, 2001).

63. See, for example, René Girard, *Violence and the Sacred,* trans. Patrick Gregory (Baltimore: Johns Hopkins University Press, 1977), 17–23.

64. Martin Luther King Jr., "Letter from a Birmingham Jail," 19. http://okra.stanford.edu/transcription/document_images/undecided/630416-019.pdf.

65. Ibid., 10.

innocent to further injustice; it is not a good, but it reveals the injustice of what is called "order" in an unjust society. According to King, such civil disobedience "was practiced superbly by the early Christians who were willing to face hungry lions and the excruciating pains of chopping blocks, before submitting to certain unjust laws of the Roman empire."[66]

In Moss's view, as we have seen, the persecution or prosecution of Christians by the Romans was an attempt to maintain social cohesiveness. Christians' attempts to question the justice of the social order were naturally suppressed as subversive; Christians were not seen as heroic, to say the least. According to Moss, "Prior to Christianity, being persecuted was a sign either of one's own moral failings or that one's deity was weak, angry, or indifferent."[67] Girard could not have said it better himself. Before Christianity, society maintained social cohesion by blaming the victim; Christianity, for the first time, reveals the injustice and falsehood of the scapegoating mechanism.

Moss decries the way that Christianity has made persecution into a marker of moral righteousness: "because of this, the claim that one experiences persecution actually becomes a way of acquiring political and cultural power," even outside of Christian circles.[68] Moss is right that our concern should be directed toward others, not claiming victim status for ourselves as a way of attaining power; Girard would certainly agree. Girard, indeed, has pointed to the way that claiming victim status for oneself has become a new way of scapegoating others in a society that has been influenced by Christianity's valorization of the victim.[69] As Girard has commented, "Never before in history have people spent so much time throwing victims at one another's heads as a substitute for other weapons. This can only happen in a world that though far from Christian to be sure, is totally permeated by the values of the gospels."[70] But Girard's central insight is about how worshipping a crucified God turns the social order upside down; we now view the world from the point of view of the lowly and downtrodden, those who are said to be marginalized because they deserve it. Girard considers the

66. Ibid., 9.

67. Moss, *Myth of Persecution*, 254.

68. Ibid., 254–55.

69. See, for example, Girard, *I See Satan*, 161–69, and René Girard, *Evolution and Conversion: Dialogues on the Origins of Culture* (London: Continuum, 2008), 257–58.

70. René Girard, "Generative Scapegoating," in Robert Hamerton-Kelly, ed., *Violent Origins: Walter Burkert, René Girard, and Jonathan Z. Smith on Ritual Killing and Cultural Formation* (Stanford: Stanford University Press, 1987), 140.

weaponization of victimhood as a distortion of the gospel in a society that is insufficiently Christian, not a pathology at the heart of the gospel itself.

It is not good to be persecuted, nor is marginalization necessarily a sign of moral righteousness. Following a crucified God does mean, however, that we should not expect to have power and prestige. If Christians are faithful and see Jesus in the hungry, the sick, and the imprisoned, we can expect not to fit neatly into any social order maintained by their marginalization. We need to give up the Constantinian habit of expecting a privileged place in a Christian country. We should claim the freedom to practice our faith and rejoice when we have it, but not attempt to reclaim some lost cultural hegemony. *Pace* the bishops, sometimes one *does* have to choose between being Christian and being American. We should not expect to fit neatly into the American social order, either by having our beliefs enshrined in law or by privatizing our faith so that we can get along with those who do not share it. Christians are not always and everywhere persecuted, but we need to remember that, short of the eschaton, there is always tension between the city of God and the earthly city.

2

St. Augustine on the Church as Sacrifice, Then and Now

Paige E. Hochschild

St. Augustine's City of God has long been a classic text for reflection upon "realistic engagement" between Christians and the earthly city, which is their home but not their final end. This paper considers engagement in light of Augustine's claim that it is the essence and vocation of the church to become the "living temple and sacrifice" of God.[1] City of God, written toward the end of Augustine's life, speaks to Roman Christians who are far from an "emerging minority," and yet who are deeply imbedded in Roman imperial culture and therefore called to give an account of their apparent complicity in its decline. The response given by Augustine is remarkable: to the accusation that the Christian prohibition of sacrifice to traditional Roman gods has contributed to Rome's political failures, Augustine writes in order to articulate the true form of the "city of God," by establishing true piety (vera pietas) and the worship of God (Dei cultus).[2] Augustine writes City of God for a diverse audience; nevertheless, by reading the contemporary "signs of the times" in light of history, revelation, and rational argument, Augustine writes with greatest urgency to the church.[3] The form

---

1. De civitate Dei 12.9 (CCL 47), in the translation of Henry Bettenson (London: Penguin Classics, 1972).

2. Civ. 1.36.

3. On the seeds of civ. present in ep. 137 and 138, and locating the dedication of civ. to Marcellinus in relation to his role at the Conference of Carthage (in 411), see Giuseppe Visonà, "Il De Civitate Dei e l'Epistolario di Agostino," in Lettura del De Civitate Dei Libri I-X. Lectio Augustini XV-XVI-XVII: Settimana Agostiniana Pavese 1999–2001, Studia

of true piety and right worship of God should delineate what it looks like for the church to be "in the world," in a mode of "realistic engagement." By calling the church to be a living temple and sacrifice to God, Augustine teaches the grave responsibility of the church to complete the sacrificial work of Christ's mediation, beginning from the common bond of human solidarity under sin.[4] Insofar as Christians are members of the earthly city, they must identify and proclaim this common state of servitude, and be a living witness against a universal tendency to idolatry; they must be able to enact right worship in a visible and public way, in accordance with the sacrificial dimension of all *religio*; and they must persevere in the virtues proper to hope and the hard labor of completing the body of Christ in history. This paper considers the importance of the treatment of sacrifice at the heart of *City of God*, arguing that sacrifice, rightly understood, provides the logic of these three aspects of the church's vocation. Finally, this paper concludes by suggesting contemporary implications of the sacrificial form of the church, with the assistance of recent theologically influential Augustianians: Congar, Daniélou, and Ratzinger.

Sacrifice in *De Civitate Dei* 10

The immediate context for the discussion of sacrifice in the tenth book is anthropological. Augustine opens with the great question of ancient ethics: What is happiness? Can human fulfillment actually be enjoyed in this present life? Augustine observes that philosophy has provided an answer: Plato says that the best life is the one lived in accordance with virtue, and that virtue is only possible with the "knowledge of God," by imitation *of* God or participation *in* God.[5] To the question of attainment, the Platonic tradition, represented in "modern times" by Plotinus, Iamblichus, Apuleius, and Porphyry, advocates a *via* contrary to its explicit response to the question of happiness: the worship (*colere*) of many gods, by means (*honores, sacrificia*) entirely inappropriate to created beings.[6] Augustine restricts *true* happi-

---

Ephemeridis Augustinianum 96 (Rome: Institutum Patristicum Augustinianum, 2003) 7–32.

4. Romans 3:23, cited by Augustine at *s.* 80.4.

5. *Civ.* 8.8; 10.1.

6. Ibid., 8.12. Compared to cult of martyrs, cf. 8.27; on the ordering of the community of the angels to the worship of the one God and for confirming faith by miracles, cf. 8.25; 10.7–8. On the complexity of Augustine's relationship to this tradition, see Stéphane Toulouse, "Que le Vrai Sacrifice est Celui d'un Coeur Pur," in *Recherches Augustiniennes*

ness, the fulfillment of all human longings, to the "divine life": revelation and ancient wisdom appear to confirm one another.[7] With characteristic realism, Augustine admits that the question of the *via* is disputed among philosophers, and thus it is more "probable that people, simply by virtue of being mortal," are bound to be "wretched" in this life.[8] The possibility and form of *present* happiness remains on the table, given the argument of the first five books of *City of God* that the worship of demons, idolatry in general, or a civil theology detached from sound natural theology generate misery for individuals and discord in the earthly city. If true happiness is a property of the divine life, while remaining a fulfillment of ordinary human desires, the climax of books 6–10 must offer an account adequate to both: effective mediation of the divine life reconciled together with the mortality that defines the human condition, in the unity of a single principle.[9] Book 10 is about effective mediation, which confers both present benefits and eternal felicity. As an eschatological promise, mediation is effective if it confers happiness with permanence and stability; as a present reality, mediation is effective by divine indwelling, which is in turn made visible in the fulfilling of the commandment to love God and neighbor. Christ perfects what is properly human by being a true mediator (*verus mediator*). The oneness of his person is evidence that ontologically divergent principles are united through divine initiative. It is not simply by being the divine word that mediation is effective, but rather by "sharing in" humanity as a

---

32 (2001) 169–223, especially his thematic conclusion on p. 221.

7. Ibid., 9.15; this argument is developed from the early works through to *De Trinitate* (CCL 50/50a; cf. 8.6–12): see for example, *c. acad.* 1.3.9; 1.8.23, and *b. vita* 4.33 (CCL 29); arguably, *De vera religione* is a complete argument on mediation of the divine life through history, revelation, and reason. "True" qualifying happiness suggests "fullness" or perfection; thus a partial but imperfect happiness prior to a perfect state is possible. However, in posing the question of the "right way," Augustine incorporates a sense of "true" that is simply opposed to the false: a false end (or good) cannot promise any kind of true good, nor a true way; cf. *conf.* 10.21.30—23.34; Guy de Broglie, "La notion augustinienne du sacrifice 'invisible' et 'vrai,'" *Recherches de Science Religieuse* 48 (1960) 135–60.

8. *Civ.* 9.15.

9. Ibid., 9.15. Augustine writes in the immediate context of the renewed push to restore Roman sacrifice, and the most intelligent rationale for sacrifice is found among the disciples of Porphyry who advocate continuity with civic laws and customs, and commend nonanimal sacrifice in order to show gratitude by first-fruit offering and a purified "character" (Porphyry, *De Abstinentia* 2.14–15; 19; 34–35); cf. Frances M. Young, *The Use of Sacrificial Ideas in Greek Christian Writers from the New Testament to John Chrysostom* (Cambridge, MA: The Philadelphia Patristic Foundation, 1979), 27.

compendium of the human condition.[10] In book 10, Augustine emphasizes a further point: Christ is an effective, or true, mediator by being "the unique sacrifice."[11] This shifts the focus away from the more abstract question of contact between the intelligible and the physical, back to the central question of true worship moving books 1–8.

Religiosity arises from human nature, particularly its social dimension, and thus falls under the virtue of justice. Justice, in the juridical sense, describes what is owed to God alone in respect of his nature; in the properly moral sense, justice (like the other cardinal virtues) is not only a habit for Augustine, but a form, conferring a stable, perfective quality upon a person. The form of all virtue is divine charity.[12] Augustine links the juridical and the moral senses of justice by locating justice essentially in the divine nature; if God is perfectly just, human justice in relation to God is both a "rendering of what is due" to God (charity), and a moral conformity to God by imitation of God (as charity itself).[13] Augustine must bring clarity to the language of *religio* and *sacrificium* in order to differentiate justice as it pertains to God from justice as it pertains to other creatures. The first half of *City of God* 10 considers miracles, theophanies, and the ministry of angels as manifestations of divine power and in service to divine providence.[14] Spiritual beings, good by nature and by disposition, do not claim worship as their due; instead, they serve the will of God, thereby directing all *religio* to God: "their aim is our blessedness, and therefore they wish us not to sacrifice to themselves, but to God."[15] Justice ordains that creatures

10. *Civ.* 9.15: a bad mediator "separates friends" (*qui separat amicos*), while a good mediator "reconciles what is opposed" (*qui reconciliat inimicos*).

11. Ibid., 10.20; cf. "unus mediator" at 9.15; "illo sacrificio singulari" at 4.31 and 7.31.

12. *De moribus ecclesiae catholicae* 15.24 (CSEL 90); *Civ.* 15.22; cf. F. J. Thonnard, "Justice de Dieu et justice humaine selon saint Augustin," in *Augustinus* 12 (1967) 387–402.

13. *Ep.* 120.4 (CSEL 34.2, 704–22): "Cogitemus nos potius tanto similiores Deo, quanto esse poterimus eius participatione iustiores."

14. I am loosely dividing *Civ.* 10 into two parts: chs. 1–19 and chs. 20–32, with two christological passages forming the central thematic bridge, chs. 6 and 20. If the first half handles sacrifice under the rubric of right *religio*, completing the apologetic of the first nine books by arguing for the right end of worship and the right *via* of sacrifice (and note that the name of Christ occurs only once in these chapters [at 10.6], in reference to a citation from Romans 12:5), the second half focuses on Christ ("homo Christus Iesus") as *ille verus mediator*, and his effecting of a) eternal life/happiness (viz. eschatological promise) and b) purgation (viz. well-being in present life).

15. *Civ.* 10.7.

not be worshipped, but only God; nor is this needed by God as though he lacked any thing, but rather because worship orders the creature rightly in relation to God.

A term such as "worship" (*cultus, colere*) is ambiguous with respect to its object, describing a relation to God, to an institution or to a person.[16] Piety (*pietas*) commonly describes filial bonds while retaining a wider flexibility. Even religion itself (*religio*) can describe being "bound" to other persons or practices, and it can therefore remain a natural or moral virtue with multiple possible referents. Augustine forces etymological complexity on the term *religio*. Normally, he understands it as a "binding" (from *religare*), but at 10.3 he proposes another derivation from *religentes*, a choosing or loving.[17] The dual etymology allows Augustine, once again, to elide philosophical wisdom (the end of "clinging to God") with revelation, specifically the commandment to love God and neighbor, because "in choosing God, we approach him through love, so that, when we reach him, we may rest in him, blessed because made perfect by the attainment of our end." Further, one is led to this good, and leads others to this good, because love of one's own good implies a good common to all people. Like Tertullian before him, Augustine removes ambiguity from *religio* by arguing that *religio* is only true and universal, genuinely perfecting of human longing, when it has a single, unique, and divine end.[18]

"Choosing" and "being bound" implies both human initiative and divine grace. Augustine understands *religio* as architectonic—that is, it pertains to ordering all aspects of human life under and in relation to God as final end. Augustine treats sacrifice within this binding and architectonic

---

16. Ibid.,10.1.

17. At *retr.* 1.13.19 (CCL 57), Augustine concludes that *religio* comes from *religare*. It is important, in the context of Donatism in North Africa, that his etymological moves in *Civ.* 10 incorporate a passive dimension (implying the grace of faith) and an active one (implying the whole of Christian life as an ordering of loves). It is tempting to analyze the dual etymology in light of Thonnard's approach to justice for Augustine.

18. "True" as opposed to false; cf. note 7. This point, argued at 10.3, truly completes the argument of *Civ.* 1–9. Tertullian argues that Christianity is a *religio*, derived from Judaism, and therefore, building upon the unique status of Judaism in the Roman Empire, approximating the form of a *religio* (*Apol.* 21). To the Romans, he writes: "if their gods do not exist," they have no *religio* (24). Christians are therefore innocent of impiety or treason against religion; rather, the Romans are guilty of both by refusing *true religion* and "worshipping a lie instead." On the developing sense of *religio* and its opposition to *superstitio* in the 2nd–3rd c., see Maurice Sachot, "Comment le Christianisme est-il Devenu *Religio*?," in *Revue des Sciences Religieuses* 59.2 (1985) 95–118.

sense of religion. Sacrifice is a part of religion by particularizing the right ordering of all created things in relation to God.[19] Augustine offers a definition of sacrifice: "every work done in order that we might cling to God in holy fellowship, that is, every work (*opus*) which is referred to the final good in which we are truly blessed."[20] This definition is vague, but it allows Augustine to introduce the sacrifice of Christ as the locus of effective mediation indirectly, with a clear ecclesiological focus. *City of God* 10.6 and 10.20 form a christological bridge for 10, and thus merit clearer analysis: the argument of 10.6 gives specificity to the general initial definition of *verum sacrificium* as "*omne opus*." It is possible to read *City of God* 10.6 as an exegesis of Romans 12:1–6a in light of sacrifice as a fundamental ecclesial characteristic:

1) true sacrifice is effected (*agitur*) in every work that unites one in holy fellowship with God (*sancta societate inhaereamus Deo*), and thereby in true happiness

   a. this is a "divine matter" (*res divina*), even if done by man

   b. this is an act of "compassion" (*misericordia*), an act of self-care, and good for man

2) example: body made a sacrifice, when disciplined by temperance (*cum temperantia castigamus*); cf. Rom. 6:16 ("*hostiam vivam*" as "reasonable offering")

   a. according to measure (*quem ad modum debemus*)—viz. *iustitia* of God

   b. for the sake of God

3) example: soul made a sacrifice, when it offers itself to God (*se refert ad Deum*)

   a. kindled by the fire of love

---

19. *Civ.* 10.6. *De vera religione* (CCL 32) 37.68—40.76 describes reestablishing the right relation of things to God as a correction of "impiety" by true worship (*colere*) and service (*servitus*). The threefold action at *civ.* 10.6 recalls the threefold form of the "slavery of sin" at *vera rel.* 38.69 from 1 John 2:16. At *doctr. Chr.* 1.17.16, the way to blessedness is described as a *via* of the "affections" or (1.22.20—26.27) of a restored order of loves viz. self, neighbor, and creation under and in relation to God. In particularizing religion, sacrifice describes the visibility of worship: cf. *Civ.* 19.21, where Augustine speaks of the gods the Romans "worshipped with sacrifice."

20. *Civ.* 10.6.

>b. losing the form (*forma*) of worldly desire (*concupiscentia secularis*)[21]

c. re-formed in subordination to, in likeness to, the unchanging form of God (*tamquam incommutabili formae subdita reformetur*)

4) *Conclusion I* (making "works" more specific): true sacrifices (*vera sacrificia*) are acts of compassion (*misericordia*) viz. self or neighbor, which liberate from misery (*a miseria*) and bring one to happiness (*adhaerere Deo*)

5) Therefore ("*profecto efficitur*"), the "whole redeemed community" (*civitas*), the "congregation and fellowship of the saints," is the *sacrificium universale*

a. through the "great priest" who *offers*: so that we might be united with him, as a body to its head

b. through the sacrifice offered, *in passione*: so that we might be an "acceptable sacrifice to God," having become (in union with Christ) the "whole sacrifice" (*totum sacrificium*)

6) *Conclusion II*: the "sacrifice of Christians" (*sacrificium Christianorum*) is the enacting and completing of Christ's own unity (offering/offered) in the church

The sacrament of the altar, Augustine says, is the privileged place where the church is shown (*ubi ei demonstratur*) what it is. Human agency and the grace of divine compassion coincide in the church's offering to the one God, by which, united to Christ mediating in the *forma servi*, the church itself becomes the sacrifice offered.

It is misleading to read this text as primarily concerned with the Eucharist as sacrifice: while three elements are clearly connected—the sacrifice of Christ (*verum sacrificium*), the sacrifice of the body of Christ/of Christians (*sacrificium totum, universale*), and the sacrament of the altar—the emphasis is ecclesial. The *universality* of sacrifice responds to the universality of the *via* for which the Platonists sought, albeit without success: thus Augustine argues briefly, at 10.24 and at 10.32, that Christ's lineage from the seed of Abraham, "by birth a Chaldean" and yet compelled to leave

---

21. *Forma* is a central Christological term in *De vera religione* (CCL 32), linking the creative activity of the *logos* with the salvific activity of the mediator (cf. 11.21; 12.24; 18.35; 40.74; 44.82; 55.113); *misericordia* is a term for grace in the order of providence, cf. 8.14; 10.19.

his country and family to receive the promise of the "universal way," does not restrict the mediation of this "way" to one nation or people.[22] Roland Teske observes that language describing particular sacrificial acts, such as "consecration by God's name," recall baptismal language.[23] The chapter that forms the other side of the christological bridge of *City of God* 10, chapter 20, explicitly refers to the Eucharist as the "daily *sacramentum*" of the church's sacrifice.[24] Nevertheless, the dual focus on Jesus Christ as sacrifice/priest-sacrificing and church as sacrifice/sacrificing in 10.20 is even stronger. At 10.20, Augustine locates the mediating work of Christ in the logic of Trinitarian love, and the primary effect of Christ's priestly sacrifice is the incorporation of the church as his own body.

The Word of God, in whom all things have been created, "reaches out" and unites the human condition to itself, in time.[25] This "reaching" is not identical with the eternal Trinitarian mission of divine persons. Remaining at all times the Word, the "form of God" (*forma Dei*) is never abandoned; nevertheless, insofar as the Trinitarian love between Father and Son is the *ratio* for both creation and salvation, the particular *work* of "assuming" (*adsumere*) human nature is explained by the motive cause of Trinitarian love.[26] Rather than offering multiple, purifying "principles"

22. Augustine emphasizes the universality of Christ's mediation by linking him historically with Melchizedek, and linking a priestly people with the promises to Abraham; cf. *Civ.* 17.5: "Doubtless by 'priesthood' he means the people itself, the people whose priest is the mediator between God and men, the man Jesus Christ" (trans. Bettenson).

23. "The Definition of Sacrifice in the *De Civitate Dei*," in Douglas Kries and Catherine Brown Tkacz, eds., *Nova Doctrina Vetusque: Essays on Early Christianity in Honor of Fredric W. Schlatter, S.J.* (New York: Peter Lang, 1999) 153–68.

24. A sentence with more than one possible translation (cf. note 29), but a clear meaning given that "res" clearly refers to the sacrifice of Christ as priest and offering: "Cuius rei sacramentum cotidianum esse voluit ecclesiae sacrificium." A good balance of the two senses of sacrifice (Christ and the church) and the sacrament of the altar is found in Daniel Jones, "The *Verum Sacrificium* of Christ and Christians in *De Civitate Dei* 10: Eucharist, Christology and Christian Identity," in Gerard Deighan, ed., *Celebrating the Eucharist: Sacrifice and Communion*, Fota Liturgy Series 5 (Wells, Somerset: Smenos, 2014), 135–72. Although he must go beyond *Civ.* 10 to articulate the sacrificial dimension of the Eucharist as such, Jones does this by rightly focusing on the priesthood of the ascended Christ and the "mutual inherence" of Christ and the church in the sacraments. This argument would be enriched by the weight that Augustine places in the later books of *civ.* on the supplanting of the Aaronic priesthood by that of Melchizedek (the eternal priesthood, in which Jesus Christ happens to share).

25. *Civ.* 10.24: *Haec est mediatio, qua manus lapsis iacentibusque porrecta est.*

26. On Trinitarian soteriology, see Robert Dodaro, "Augustine on the Roles of Christ and the Holy Spirit in the Mediation of Virtues," *Augustinian Studies* 41.1 (2010) 145–63.

(as the Platonists do), Christ is the singular principle; insofar as he is the divine Word, through whom "all things are created," he has power (to give life; to purify).[27] Uniting with flesh, becoming one person, Christ appears in the "form of a servant" (*forma servi*). The sense of "appearing" implied by *forma* is strongly nondocetic: if the purpose of "assuming" is purification, Augustine is clear that flesh in itself cannot purify. Only the power of God (as *principium*), united with flesh, can conquer the moral and ontological corruptibility that marks the human condition.[28]

In the *forma servi*, Christ "prefers" to be the sacrifice offered (*sacrificium maluit esse*), and the high priest offering sacrifice.[29] Christ's priestly sacrificial action, associated with his humanity, accomplishes reconciliation with God: through his sacrificial *opus* (in *forma servi*), Christ mediates (as *unus Christus*).[30] Augustine emphasizes the *freedom* of Christ's self-gift, and the *active work* of the one sacrificing. At 10.20, Augustine says that the historical event of Christ's sacrifice is the *res*, the *verum sacrificium*, to which the daily *sacramentum* of the church refers, so that the church, "the body of this head," might learn from "this" to offer itself "through him."[31] What does the daily sacrament teach (*discit*) the church? The church learns what it is and what it must become: a sacrificial body, offered to God through Christ the mediator, and a freely sacrificing, priestly people in the world. Augustine reads sacred history as a pedagogy serving this end, as he will argue in books 15–19 in greater detail: all the sacrifices of saints "in early times" were *signa* of the true sacrifice, and they prefigure it as "many words" can

27. *Civ.* 10.24.

28. Cf. John 6:57, cited at 10.24: "'It is the spirit which gives life; the flesh is of no help.' The *principium*, having assumed a soul and flesh, purifies the soul and flesh of believers." See also 10.27, where Christ brings about "purification full of compassion" namely "the purification of mind, spirit and body"; in order to accomplish this, he must take up (*suscepit*) the whole of human nature ("...*totum hominem*"). At 10.25, Augustine uses Psalm 73 to link the faith of the psalmist with the eschatological hope of Christians: "though he has spoken of the failure of both heart and flesh, he does not add, 'God of my heart and flesh', but 'God of my heart'. For it is clearly by means of the heart that the flesh is purified."

29. *Civ.* 10.20: *ipse offerens, ipse et oblatio.*

30. Cf. *Io. eu. tr.* 108. 5 (CCEL 36.618). The distinction and relation of mediation and priesthood is important for Augustine's soteriology and, in conversation with Donatists, his ecclesiology. While mediation is attributed to the whole person of the Incarnate Christ, priestly intercession and sacrifice is particularly attributed to the *forma servi*, and by extension to the church; cf. Joseph Carola, *Augustine of Hippo: The Role of the Laity in Ecclesial Reconciliation* (Rome: Editrice Pontificia Università Gregoriana, 2005), 197.

31. *Civ.* 10.20.

refer to one thing. God has "never failed to instruct" his people, through angels, through the Law, and then the prophets: all of sacred history "announces" (*preadicata est*) the same promise: the "worship of the one God" and the "coming of his mediator."[32]

The unity of the person of Jesus Christ is clearly central to the salvation-historical argument of *City of God*. In *The Trinity* 4, Augustine shows by biblical and logical *convenientia* that Christ's incarnation is an appropriate and effective way of mediation: the (a) unity (*unum*) of Father and Son, and of humanity united with Christ, as well as the (b) historical-providential unity (*unus*) of Christ as contrasted with the temporal multiplicity of creation, describe two senses of "unity" (or oneness) linked by the salvific action of Christ's mediation.[33] In *City of God* 10, the Son *receives* sacrifice in unity with God the Father, to whom alone sacrifice can be justly given. Christ *offers* sacrifice as a man—"through which he willed to be also a priest"—thereby embodying the perfect form of *religio* as a referring of all things to God in love, and completing the historical argument of the "eternal priesthood" founded in Melchizedek, supplanting the priesthood of Aaron, and ended in Christ's priestly work.[34] Finally, Christ *is offered* as the "unique sacrifice"—"unique" as a matter of history because the many sacrifices (*multiplicia*) refer to him as signs to the thing itself (*res*); "unique" as a matter of "true religion" because he is offered to God, whereas false sacrifices are marked by the diversity of form, temple, and altar required by many gods (*multos deos . . . congregaverat*).[35] Christ is also the "unique"

32. Ibid., 10.25; 10.24.

33. Isabelle Bochet, "The Hymn to the One in Augustine's *De Trinitate* IV," *Augustinian Studies* 38.1 (2007) 41–60; see also *Confessiones*, 10.39.40; 11.29.39. On the anti-Homoian polemic of *trin.* 1–4, see Michel Barnes, "Exegesis and Polemic in Augustine's *De Trinitate* I," *Augustinian Studies* 30 (1999) 43–59.

34. Augustine, like Ambrose and Cyprian, locates a prefiguring of Christ's priestly office in Melchizedek—a man, Augustine observes, both priest and king, and yet, appropriately, lacking temple or kingdom. For Ambrose, cf. *De sacramentiis* 4.3.10–12; 5.1.1 (SC 25bis 106–8; 120); Cyprian, *Ep.* 63 4.1 (CSEL 3.2). Augustine is explicit about using *Hebrews* as a source for his treatment of Melchizedek (*Civ.* 16.22; 17.5); on the significance of the Latin biblical text, see Gerald Bonner, "The Doctrine of Sacrifice: Augustine and the Latin Patristic Tradition," in S. W. Sykes, ed., *Sacrifice and Redemption: Durham Essays in Theology* (Cambridge: Cambridge University Press, 1991), 101–17; Robert J. Miller, *Helping Jesus Fulfill Prophecy* (Eugene, OR: Wipf and Stock, 2015), 286–96. On Christ as the "high priest," see 10.6 ("…per sacerdotum magnum"); cf. also 10.3; 10.17, where Hebrew sacrifice is ordained to be changed for something better, through the action of a "better priest" ("per meliorem sacerdotem"); 10.20; 10.22; 10.31.

35. *Civ.* 3.12. These sacrifices are "false" because they are not offered to the "one God";

sacrifice as a matter of effectiveness: although Christ claims the unlikeness of being morally blameless, he is in every other aspect united to humanity, in solidarity, for the express purpose of removing this unlikeness.

What the church sees and learns is not merely visual or symbolic. The true sacrifice is the *opus* of Christ accomplished once in history: the "Son of God, while remaining unchangeably in his own proper being, clothed himself in humanity and gave to men the spirit of love by the mediation of a man."[36] Knowing God to be the one true God whose nature as Trinitarian love inclines him to reach out to "wretched beings," the church learns that it owes God its complete service as a just return.[37] The *opera* of Christians is the self-offering, in and through Christ's *opus* as priest/sacrifice, of all things back to God. The primary effect of Christ's work is unification: the church constituted as the temple of God. We are his temple, Augustine says at *City of God* 10.3, all at the same time (*simul*), and individually, because God "deigns to inhabit" each person in the "concord of all." Individually and corporately, the heart lifted up becomes his altar; propitiation is made through his "only-begotten priest"; victims are sacrificed in the witness to the truth; incense is burned in the fire of "pious and holy love." Most importantly, "we are purified" of sin and evil desires, consecrated "in God's name" in order to cleave to God (*cohaerere*), and in cleaving to God, the soul is made "rich in true virtues." Augustine immediately invokes the double commandment to love God and neighbor as summative, since it is only through the corporate attainment of union with God that "true worship, religion, and piety" toward God is fulfilled.

The idea of sacrifice in 10.6 as a work (*opus*), primarily the "work of mercy" of Christ's salvation, is made concrete in the idea of the church unified by incorporation into Christ's own person—the *Christus totus*.[38] The church must be the sacrifice of Christ in the world, extending his singular work throughout history, in both an active, priestly dimension and in a

---

cf. 10.13; 10.14; 10.16; 10.17; or, as a generic construction ("*unum Deum*") contrasted to idolatry, 10.16; 10.25; 10.32. At *civ.* 7.32, Augustine allows even pagan sacrifice (as *latreia*) to be understood as "significata et praenuntiata" of Christ's sacrifice.

36. *Civ.* 10.29 (trans. Bettenson).

37. Ibid., 10.3.

38. Both a divine and a human work, because Christ is the divine Word assuming *totus homo*; cf. *s.* 293.7 (PL 38.1332). Carola observes that incorporation into Christ's humanity in no way suppresses "the subjective multiplicity of the ecclesial body" (188); cf. Michel Reveillaud, "Le Christ-Homme, tête de l'Église: Étude d'ecclésiologie selon les *Ennarationes in Psalmos* d'Augustin," *Recherches Augustiniennes* 5 (1968) 94.

passive, offering dimension. The "congregation and fellowship of the saints" becomes the "universal sacrifice" by its unity, joined as a body to Christ its head; the unity accomplished by Christ's *opus* in turn is realized in time by the sacrificial "works of mercy" which unite the members one to another in love.

Augustine frequently articulates the radical unity of Christ and the church. Writing on Psalm 61, he identifies the person of Jesus Christ with the person of the church: the suffering of Christ *is* the suffering of Christians; the suffering of Christians completes what is "lacking" in the suffering of Christ. This is signified by the "thirst of Christ" which is also the ongoing thirst of the church, a thirsting for righteousness as it endures, with patience and hope, the trials of daily life.[39] Preaching to the newly baptized (in *s.* 229), Augustine offers the Eucharist as a demonstration of unity: "Because he suffered for us, he left us the sacrament of his body and blood... for we have become his body, and through his mercy we are what we receive."[40] Marking baptism as the decisive point of joining the one body, he describes initiation using the destructive and creative imagery of baking bread: "just as you see that the bread which was made is one mass, so may you also be one body by loving one another, by . . . undivided charity." Reconciliation is the central action in this process, liturgically and in daily life, since the forgiveness of sins is the chief evidence of Christian love. Augustine enjoins humility (in *s.* 226), asking his congregation to "reflect" on their sins, for they were darkness and "are now light." By the Lord's Prayer and the "kiss of peace," peace is "made in your conscience." Therefore, "do not withdraw your heart from your neighbor." Ponder what does not pass away (as do the Eucharistic elements), "so that you may possess unity in your heart, so that you may always lift up your heart." Finally, in *s.* 227, Augustine asks the newly baptized to "focus attention on the Scriptures"; but they must also remember that "*we* are your books."[41] The bread of the Eucharist adjures the cherishing of unity. As many grains are ground up, by humiliation of

39. *En. Ps.* 61.2; 6; 15 (CCL 39).

40. Cf. *Io. eu. tr.* 98.6, on how the "transposition" of humanity into Christ's humanity applies to both mature (*spiritales*) and new Christians (*parvuli*). On the *totus Christus* as the "very atmosphere" for preaching and biblical exegesis, see Michael Cameron, "*Totus Christus* and the Psychagogy of Augustine's Sermons," *Augustinian Studies* 36.1 (2005) 59–70.

41. Italics mine; *S.* 226, 227 (PL 38: 1098–2001); *s.* 229 (cf. Denis 6) (PL 38:1103); trans. Mary Sarah Muldowney, Fathers of the Church (New York: Catholic University of America Press, 1959).

fasting and exorcism, by the water of baptism and the fire of the Holy Spirit through chrism, Christians have "become bread."

The unity that comes through reconciliation is described as purification in *s.* 227. Purification is the chief spiritual effect of Christ's sacrifice in *City of God*, and the paired terms "healed and cleansed" recur throughout that text. To the partial anthropology of Porphyry, which promised at best illumination of the intellectual soul, the effect of Christ the "whole man" is offered as a purification of the whole person. The universality of the church's membership, at least potentially, corrects the Porphyrian restriction of illumination to a select few.[42] The way that shares in Christ's sacrificial reconciliation is the "royal way" because it is the only way that effectively mediates the divine life, thereby granting the church a share in Christ's own authority. It is the "universal way" because it is open to all, and entered into from a place of solidarity in common human weakness.

Conclusions and Contemporary Implications

We can conclude by drawing out clearly the three aspects of the church's vocation to be the "universal sacrifice" completing Christ's own *opus* in the world. The church's work is an effective extension of Christ's mediation insofar as it secures both temporal and eternal felicity as they are linked within the person of Christ. The foundational mark of the church, unity, is the practical and theological foundation for two further aspects: visibility and the particular form of Christian virtue.

Unity

Incorporation into the very person of Jesus Christ is primarily a work of divine grace. Unity should be evident and ecclesial, despite the fact that its historical incompleteness can be explained by the dependence of providence upon human agency, and by the mysterious character of eschatological fulfillment.[43] Against the Porphyrian rejection of the humility of the way of Christ, the church preaches the shared bondage of humanity

---

42. *Civ.* 10.29; 10.32.

43. In respect to the Donatist controversy, see Adam Ployd, *Augustine, the Trinity, and the Church* (Oxford: Oxford University Press, 2015), 144–85; in anti-Pelagian context, see Anthony Dupont, *Gratia in Augustine's Sermones ad Populum During the Pelagian Controversy* (Leiden: Brill, 2013), 355 (on *s.* 181, as an example).

under sin, the liberation promised by the universal way (purification and healing), and through this, the fulfillment of the universal human desire for true felicity—founded in the "desire for blessedness and immortality" present even in human nature, according to Augustine.[44] Corporate unity is therefore the first attribute of the form of "true worship." Subordination (or sacrifice) of self to God and to neighbor mitigates the universal tendency of human community to idolatry, given the reality of sin and the temptation to self-sufficiency that marks the Roman ethical tradition.[45]

One contemporary implication of Augustine's connection between unity in the church and its sacrificial character as the body of Christ naturally concerns evident divisions that exist among Christians. With respect to ecumenism, one could read Augustine as offering an exhortation with a caution: true unity is primarily a divine work, and any merely human unity not predicated on a radical sense of dependence on divine action in history cannot be lasting. Catholic theologian Yves Congar, OP, draws from *City of God* 10 a different teaching on the grave responsibility of the church to be more deeply unified through an internal, spiritual renewal. Originally published in 1953, *Lay People in the Church* offers an ecclesiological vision founded in Augustine's treatment of the sacrificial character of the church.[46] To the laity, Congar particularly addresses his account of the priestly character of the church as the "new Israel," in order to find expiatory value in worship and in all aspects of Christian life. He takes Augustine's broad definition of sacrifice as a divine work and also "every work" ordered to God as end, and finds therein a "dialectic of progress at the heart of the prophet's mission," entailing a conformity of spiritual righteousness and works of mercy which in turn constitutes the people of God as a *totum sacrificium*.[47] Without eliding the distinct character and function of the ministerial priesthood, Congar argues that sacrificial mediation is the central principle of a "mystical body of Christ" ecclesiology; moreover, the duty of mediation is accomplished through the church offering creation, its own self, and

44. *Civ.* 10.32; 10.29.

45. *Civ.* 3 attempts to chronicle how Rome adopted more and more gods over time, even though it was "happier when there were fewer" (3.12); on self-sufficiency vs. humility, see 19.4; on the offering of true worship as the mark of a truly unified community as opposed to a mere "gang," see *Civ.* 4.4. and 19.13–17.

46. Published as *Jalons pour une théologie du laicat* (Éditions du Cerf: Paris, 1953); translated by Donald Attwater (Westminster, MD: Newman, 1957).

47. Congar, *Lay People*, 117.

the whole of Christian life as an actual sacrifice to God.[48] Congar clearly wishes to extend principles of life more typically associated with religious vows by resisting a limiting of sacrificial language to eucharistic theology or a theology of priestly orders. In this, he anticipates the language of the Council of the "universal call to holiness" or perfection within the whole church (*Lumen Gentium* 5). The practical implications for a theology of the laity are profound. However, for Congar, the most significant outcome should be a greater-lived witness to the totality of the demands of true *religio*, as a result of a deeper functional and spiritual unity *within* the body of Christ. The structure and opening arguments of *Lumen Gentium*, framing the mystery of the church by the initial concept of the people of God—"a royal priesthood . . . a holy nation"—suggest that Congar's insights found a hearing within the deliberations and draftings of the Council.[49]

Visibility

The idea that sacrifice is an *opus* draws together multiple strands within *civ.* The historical pedagogy of revelation within history, particularly biblical history, is broadly visible, even as it describes a movement of spiritualizing worship. As Frances Young observes, this falls in line with a pattern of critique coming from the philosophical tradition. From Socrates to Lucian in the 2nd century AD, religious practices and the sense of the divine presupposed by them are challenged on the basis of rational reflection and pragmatic, ethical value.[50] Even Porphyry makes a clear distinction between the lesser deities to whom some sacrifices ("first fruits") are owed, and the "supreme God" who can receive no sacrifice because of its transcendence and sufficiency: this God is worshipped rightly by silence, through *apatheia* in the soul, and theoretical contemplation by the mind. Augustine takes up this critique in the problem of the disjunction between "inner" convictions and "exterior" practices, for example, in his treatment of Varro in books 4 and 6 of *City of God*. Augustine strikes a careful balance between, on the one hand, arguing for continuity of Christ's sacrifice with the priestly sacrifices

48. Ibid., 147.

49. In *My Journal of the Council* (Collegeville, MN: Liturgical, 2012), translated by Mary John Ronayne, OP, and Mary Cecily Boulding, OP, Congar suggests that his specific contribution consists in emphasizing the Pauline image of the "body of Christ" (Monday 11 March, 1963), 275.

50. Young, *The Use of Sacrificial Ideas*, 16–27.

of the Old Testament and, on the other hand, arguing for the uniqueness of Christ's sacrifice as priest offering/sacrifice offered.[51] One could describe this movement as one of *spiritualizing* worship. However, Robert Daly argues that this terminology is misleading, suggesting a "rationalizing," "humanizing," and also a "dematerializing."[52] The idea of "dematerializing" is directly contrary to the logic of the incarnation in history.[53]

Augustine first addresses the spiritualizing of sacrifice in *City of God* 10 through exegesis of Hosea 6:6 as offering not a rejection of sacrifice (in favor of mercy), but a higher standard of sacrifice—at 10.5 explained as a work of mercy and, above all, Christ's work of mercy.[54] That God himself enacts sacrifice supports the idea that God does not "require" anything of creatures. The dual example of sacrifice, that of soul and body, with the sacrifice of the church in union with Christ in the *forma servi,* is aligned in 10.6. The holism of salvation corresponds to the total demands of *religio.* Moreover, Augustine explains at 10.13–14 that divine theophany operates by a principle of pedagogy: any movement from the visible to the invisible can be explained by divine adaptation to the human condition; it does not preclude either the visibility of revelation or the public character of worship. This movement instructs worshippers of God to value higher, spiritual things over lower, corporeal things, even though all things reflect in their "form" and harmony the providence and goodness of God.[55] Implying a critique of Porphyry, Augustine says that visible sacrifices are appropriate

51. *Civ.* 15.16; 16.22; 16.32; 17.5; 17.20; on the failure of sacrifice in the absence of a king, 18.28. On propitiation, see Gerald Bonner, "The Doctrine of Sacrifice," 107.

52. *Christian Sacrifice: The Judeo-Christian Background before Origen* (Washington, DC: Catholic University of America Press, 1978), 4, citing Alfred Bertholet, "Der Sinn des kultischen Opfers," *Abhandlungen der preussischen Akademie der Wissenschaften* 2 (1942) 26–27.

53. Cf. Young, *The Use of Sacrificial Ideas,* 64. Daly's magnificent book (*Christian Sacrifice*) traces the complexity of this historical movement within biblical and intertestamental literature on sacrifice through to Origen. He finds dramatically varying positions, for example, in Justin Martyr's strong alignment of pagan sacrifice with Jewish (331; cf. *Dial.* 12.3; 15.4; *Apol.* 1.13.1), or in Clement of Rome's sense of sacrifice as institutional, "according to the will of God," and clearly spiritualized (314; *Ad. Cor.* 7.3; 52.1). Irenaeus's position that Old Testament sacrifice is a providential preparation for Christian sacrifice, both falling under the same genus, and that both are part of a historical economy serving the knowledge of God, may be provide a source for Augustine (340; *Adv. Haer.* 4.26.1; 4.31.1; 4.32.1).

54. On Hosea 6:6, see Irenaeus, *Proof* 96.

55. *Civ.* 10.14, where Plotinus's *Enn.* 3.2.13 and Matthew 6:28 are made to say the same thing.

(*congruere*) and necessary.[56] A "pure will" and "good mind" are not enough; prayer and praise involve sounds and visible gestures. While the flesh is "purified" through the heart, the way of salvation that is truly universal is through the flesh. Thus the final apologetic gesture to the disciples of Porphyry in 10.29 to 10.32 defends the evidently natural character of the union of soul and body as constituting the "full and complete" nature of the human person.[57] Purification cannot involve fleeing from bodily nature as if it were the source of evil; rather, in and through life in the body, purification is made of "the whole person," preparing the "mortal being for immortality, in all of its elements."[58] All worship accordingly involves the making-visible of faith in the whole of life; moreover, it must be corporate and public, because this process is only complete in "holy fellowship" with God and all the saints.

The question of corporate worship arises within a final polemic against Porphyry at the end of *City of God* 19. Augustine has concluded that true justice (*iustitia*) in the city requires the *ordo* of right religion: submission to God in all things, and submission of bodily life to the spiritual rule of *iustitia*.[59] Augustine finds support in Porphyry's *Philosophy from Oracles*, in a text enjoining the worship (*venerari*) of God the Father, because adoration offered to God "with justice" and "with chastity and the other virtues" will make the whole of life to be an imitative "prayer to him."[60] When a people live on the foundation of right faith, of the *iustitia* of God and not of human self-sufficiency, made "active in love" (*operatur per dilectionem*), we find a veritable commonwealth (or *populus*) in the body of Christ.[61] Divine justice provides the criterion for the "intermixing" of the two cities, and the peace desired by the pilgrims who nevertheless do not see the earthly city as final in character.[62] Divine justice provides a foundation for the common good, as well as for particular virtue; given its incomplete and

56. Ibid., 10.19.

57. Ibid., 10.29.

58. Ibid., 10.32.

59. At 19.23, described as the "soul ruling the body" or with regard to ethics in particular, "reason" having rule over vice. A correspondence can be seen with the order of submission described in 10.6.

60. Ibid., 19.23.

61. Ibid., 19.24.

62. Ibid., 19.26.

eschatological character, divine justice is completed not in the perfection of virtue, but in mercy and the forgiveness of sins.[63]

The final books of *City of God*, rather than constituting a speculation on "last things" and judgment, can be read as a pressing moral exhortation to a people sharing membership in the earthly city, and engaged in a common human battle for the victory of virtue over sin and warfare.[64] While Augustine's polemic in *City of God* 10 carefully circumscribes the "spiritualizing" of worship as nevertheless inclusive of visible works, in *City of God* 21, Augustine argues from the side of "works" that true religion demands consistency of faith and action. The fear of God and the persistence of sin serve to correct complacency and presumption, calling Christians to the hard "battle" of virtue.[65] This battle is neither private nor merely interior. Augustine recalls the double law of love that fulfills the actively sacrificial nature of the church, beginning with "works of mercy" to oneself, and extending to mercy to neighbors, by "loving Christ" in a fellow Christian.[66] Having the "right object of love" is not adequate to fulfill the justice of *religio*. *How* one loves must reveal a total consistency of "inner" faith and exterior action. The standard of love is the primacy of Christ, the true sacrifice.[67] The evidence of the right ordering of loves on the foundation of Christ is, first, a lived dependency on the mercy of grace and, second, a consistency of faith and works as "faith made active in love [and] never in wrong."[68] Visible membership, participation in the sacramental life of the church, the intercession of the saints, and even works of mercy themselves are all enjoined and beneficial to salvation; however, if a Christian does not love Christ, these works "will be burnt down."[69]

63. Ibid., 19.27.

64. Karla Pollmann argues that the rhetorical purpose of moral exhortation in *Civ.* 21–22 explains Augustine's reluctance to speculate widely about the precise nature of the postresurrection state and the divine judgment in general (21.24); cf. "Moulding the Present: Apocalyptic as Hermeneutics in *City of God* 21–22," in John Doody et al., eds., *Augustine and Apocalyptic* (Lanham, MD: Lexington, 2014), 177–92.

65. *Civ.* 21.15 implies a contrast between the lordship (dominion) of God and the domination of sin. Cf. 21.16, where evil desires are said to be defeated by the love of God, through the mediator, the man Jesus Christ.

66. Ibid., 21.27.

67. Ibid., 21.26; on "how," see 21.27 (italics mine): Si enim Christiano esurienti panem tamquam Christiano darent, profecto sibi panem iustitiae, quod ipse Christus est, non negarent; quoniam Deus, non cui detur, *sed quo animo detur*, attendit.

68. Ibid., 21.25.

69. Ibid., 21.26.

The contemporary implications are many and varied. First and fore-most, Augustine offers a timeless preaching to the church on the radical demands of discipleship. If the church is the locus of the coincidence of divine grace and the active, priestly dimension of mediation, any opposi-tion of faith and works remains untenable. In *City of God* 19, Augustine suggests a clear connection between corporate worship, reconciliation, and the justice that constitutes the church as a "people." Augustine describes Christians as a wayfaring people who nevertheless have a real interest in promoting the *pax terrena*, motivated by a concern and duty in regard to "the interests of others."[70] Nevertheless, the "impossibility of avoiding the dilemma between faith and idolatry" directly challenges the "dual anchor-age" of Christian membership; it also seriously limits the possible forms for visible, corporate witness.[71] Not surprisingly, Augustine enjoins patience and a humility founded in the sense that the righteousness of the faithful is not its own. Preaching in about 410, Augustine asks the church to be mindful of its wounds:

> Evils abound, and God has willed that evils abound. [Pray as much as you can.] If evil people did not abound, then evils would not abound. The times are evil, the times are troubled, that is what people say. Let us live good lives, and the times are good. We our-selves are the times . . . If the times are evil, it is because you are evil.[72]

Nevertheless, the church must be confidently present in the world, as Christ is present, "jostled by the crowds," even if not touched.[73] The church enacts divine justice by living out the total demands of sacrificial worship. This may bring a form of peace that is not entirely looked for, since the church is not "separate" as a community of the perfectly just, but as a corporate witness to the power of Christ's mercy in the world. With this confidence, the church must demand a space for visible witness, resist-ing a fulfillment of divine peace in political structures and solutions. The church witnesses to divine justice as an image and extension of the one

---

70. Ibid., 19.14.

71. Luigi Alici, "The Violence of Idolatry and Peaceful Coexistence: the Current Rel-evance of *civ. Dei*," *Augustinian Studies* 41.1 (2010) 217.

72. Edmund Hill and John E. Rotelle, eds. and transl., *Sermons (51–94) on the New Testament* (New York: New City, 1991), 355.

73. *S.* 62 (~407), ibid., 162.

true sacrifice, illuminating the social order from within so as to bring truly common goods to light.

As one modest example, Joseph Cardinal Ratzinger argues that the church cannot be identified with the state and remain the church; nevertheless, the church reminds the state of its nonfinality. It cannot promise redemption or the perfection of earthly happiness. The divine character of justice corrects the absolutizing tendency of the state as a form of idolatry. The church requires a visible and public space to witness and teach the common good of humanity: the ordering to transcendence that Augustine finds inscribed in the human desire for happiness; the capacity for moral and spiritual progress that delineates some kind of genuine freedom; and the dignity and ethical rationality of persons in the face of excessive confidence in technology.[74] The "first service" of the Christian faith in the public sphere, according to Ratzinger, is to proclaim liberation "from the irrationality of political myths . . . The moral thing is not adventurous moralism, which tries to mind God's business, but rather honesty, which accepts man's limits and does man's work within them."[75] If the technical structures of the political order cannot on their own liberate and perfect the human condition, the church must be reinvigorated in its teaching role, not in a mode of withdrawal or opposition, but in order to complement and redirect the service of the political order to truly human goods.

Temporal Felicity and Eschatological Hope: The Virtue of a Wayfaring People

If the final books of *City of God* offer a warning against complacency and ecclesial self-sufficiency, they also (as we have suggested in the previous section) serve as an urgent exhortation to moral virtue. The sacrificial form of virtue is explained at 10.6, by a dual correspondence to body and soul. In an early work of Augustine's, *De Beata Vita*, the virtue of temperance is described as evidence of "measure" (*modus*) in the soul; linked to *frugalitas*, the "mother of all virtues," as well as Cicero's *modestia*, temperance is also called "truth."[76] The truth of moral goodness is found perfectly in Christ, the

74. "The Biblical Aspects of the Theme of Faith and Politics: A Homily," in Michael J. Miller et al., transl., *Church, Ecumenism and Politics* (San Francisco: Ignatius, 2008), 143–47.

75. Ratzinger, "Biblical Aspects," 145.

76. CCL 29; 4.32–33; 3.18.

truth who mediates the "*summus modus*" through a Trinitarian dynamic of mission and "bringing truth into being" for the sake of liberating the soul from spiritual misery.[77] In *City of God* 10.6, temperance makes the body to be a sacrifice, through ongoing discipline according to the "measure" of God ("*castigamus . . . quem ad modum debemus*"), by ordering all actions to God as end.

The soul becomes a sacrifice by offering itself wholly to God, through love: the specific language describing this offering is that of reformation. The "form of worldly love" is lost, and the soul is reformed after the likeness of the "unchanging form of God." Augustine draws here on the strong language of *De Vera Religione*, of Christ as the exemplary form of God in creation and, in conjunction with the reconciling work of the Holy Spirit, the perfecting form of the "new man."[78] Christ's mediation is effective through the work of the divine *ars medicinae*: the "application" of the form of Christ to the person, according to the threefold structure of sin from 1 John 2:16, involves the daily "transferal of loves" from temporal things to eternal things, through temperance and justice.[79] The language of conversion and reformation takes up the passive dimension of sacrifice in *City of God* 10—the self reordered and thus offered to God—as well as the active, priestly dimension of sacrifice—the act of offering and reordering through temperance and justice. The active and passive dimensions are held together in fruitful tension by the image of the *forma servi*.

The primacy of Christ's sacrificial *opus* in *City of God* is explicitly linked to divine indwelling, again correcting the self-sufficiency of ancient virtue. Nevertheless, the urgency of tone in the final books of *City of God* and the recurring theme of the fear of God make clear that the sacrificial form of virtue entails hard labor and a grave habit of humility.[80] In the *Quaestionum Evangeliorum*, Augustine links the church at present with the eschatological church: as Martha invites Christ into her home, so the church invites

---

77. *B. vita* 4.34: "...*a quo procedit.*"

78. *Vera rel.* 55.112.

79. Ibid., 41.78; 54.104; 55.113.

80. See Augustine's *De Sermone Domini in Monte* (CCL 35), likely written in 393/395, where the virtues are classified as an interpretation of the Beatitudes at 1.3.10. Poverty of spirit is understood as the fear of God, the abiding foundation of all the virtues. The fear of God is more strongly linked to the perfection of virtue in wisdom, in s. 347.3; cf. Gerard van Riel, "La sagesse chez Augustin: de la philosophie à l'Écriture," in Isabelle Bochet, ed., *Augustin philosophe et prédicateur: Hommage à Goulven Madec* (Turnhout: Brepols, 2013), 389–405.

Christ into its heart.[81] The hard and necessary labor of Martha is the service of the church in history. Martha rightly asks for Mary's help, because she sits at the Lord's feet, receiving "the one and necessary thing"; in light of the end goal of history, when the church will enjoy the posture of Mary, the service of Martha is the necessary and good means to that restful end. The eschatological ordering of virtue establishes a living connection between the felicity of the "present struggle" and eternal felicity. The life of the resurrected body completes the logic of *religio*: the subordination of bodily life to spiritual truth; the subordination of all things to God, through Christ. The meaning of history is given dignity and value in light of its end, because the end gives architectonic, human shape to Christian hope and patience.

Jean Daniélou suggests that the church express the vocation of Martha and the sacrificial virtues of the *forma servi* by being in the world "as the poor." In a text written concurrently with the drafting of *Gaudium et Spes*, *Prayer as a Political Problem*, Daniélou echoes the thinking of Ratzinger on the church's missionary heart.[82] If Christianity is the faith of the poor, it must be truly universal in scope: accessible, deeply rooted in culture "as *religio*," and a constituent element of social life. The problem of prayer is the truly human and social problem of "space."[83] The church must work to ensure that a cultural space exists for virtue as a development of universal human desires, recognizing the natural good of religion at "the heart of the city," and on that foundation to proclaim the true God.[84] When Christians "defend God's place in the city," they do not defend God, but rather "man himself." Daniélou makes the humanistic defense more specific: to be in the world rightly is to love what is good in the world and hate what is evil. In *The Lord of History*, Daniélou explains this love as a kind of poverty, and as "the universal Christian attitude": poverty is the feeling of exile, of being "disinherited," that comes with giving oneself entirely to God while being in "the thick of battle" in order to bear "a larger share of men's troubles" out of love.[85]

---

81. CCL 44B, 2.20.

82. Jean Daniélou, *Gaudium et Spes, Prayer as a Political Problem,* edited and translated by J. R. Kirwan (Sheed and Ward: New York, 1967); originally published as *L'oraison problème politique* (Arthème Fayard: Paris, 1965).

83. Daniélou, *Prayer,* 15–18.

84. Ibid., 103–4; 109–12.

85. Jean Daniélou, *The Lord of History,* translated by Nigel Abercrombie (Longmans, Green and Co: London, 1958), 294–97; originally published as *Essai sur le Mystère de*

Poverty is a radical sense of dependence and hope; founded in right religion and devotion to God, it is spiritually fruitful of many virtues, summed up in the love of God. The "love of God" that sets the soul on fire and makes one a pleasing sacrifice to God (at *Civ.* 10.6) is the poverty of Christ offered up in the passive dimension of sacrifice. The primacy of Christ's sacrifice suggests the limit-case of the church in its call to virtue in the world: not martyrdom, per se, but the total self-offering at "the heart of the Christian mystery."[86] To close with Daniélou, arguably exegeting Augustine's full sense of sacrifice as the defining characteristic of the church:

> Everything [we have said about poverty] comes down in the end to that participation in the death and resurrection of Christ which is continually enacted in his mystical body and in each of its members. The coupling of poverty and abundance, death and life, delineates the very foundation of the Christian life, the life that is in Christ, in his death and in his resurrection. We died with him and rose again with him in baptism, and his death and resurrection will be fulfilled in us again . . . But in the meanwhile all that space of time . . . still belongs to Christ's death and resurrection. . . . Vivification is the essential thing; the point of Christianity is to release the springs of love within us . . . As St. Augustine said, if the domain of charity is to be enlarged, the domain of the flesh must be restricted: but this mortification is all for the sake of life.[87]

l'Histoire (Éditions de Seuil: Paris, 1953).

86. Daniélou, *Lord of History*, 303.

87. Ibid., 303.

3

To Be a Minority

David Novak

Old Majority—New Minority

FOR SEVEN AND A half happy years, from 1989 until 1997, I taught in the Department of Religious Studies at the University of Virginia in Charlottesville. One of my most vivid memories from that time is of the Evangelical Christian students who occasionally found their way to my door in Cocke Hall in order to pour out their hearts to me. They came to tell me how marginalized they were in their lives as definite minorities in the university. Not only did they tell me how often they had been ridiculed by their fellow students because of their practice of such things as daily prayer and Bible study, but they had been just as often ridiculed by their professors for their beliefs. Their beliefs—that is, of course, their faith—were deemed to be parochial and retrograde in the liberal culture of the contemporary academy. They told me that they came to me because I was one of the few professors at UVA who was known for having a personal religious commitment, and who would most likely be sympathetic to others having a similar commitment.

This *cri de coeur* from what could be called a "despised minority" cannot, of course, be said to be unique to the University of Virginia. It could surely be made by Evangelical students at any number of colleges and universities in North America. Nevertheless, it is especially significant considering the history of the University of Virginia. For the University of Virginia (UVA) is the first university in the United States to be without an official connection to a church.[1] In fact, UVA was founded by Thomas Jefferson, third President of the United States, who meant his university to be explicitly secular. Thus Jefferson made it quite clear at the very outset that "a professorship of theology should have no place in our institution."[2] And his spirit has lived on at UVA. So, it is no wonder that there are not too many Evangelical students at UVA, and that those who dare to come there feel as marginalized as those who found their way to my door in Cocke Hall. In fact, some of them told me that their parents and their pastors had warned them this would be the case at UVA, and who were advised to attend more "religion-friendly" schools, of which there are many, especially in the American South.

After pouring out their hearts to me for about a half hour, when some of the Evangelical students (who were usually Protestant, but sometimes Catholic) had to "come up for air" so to speak, I was finally able to say to them: "You sound like Jews." And they almost always answered: "We feel like Jews." To this I replied: "Well, we now really have something to talk about *with* each other. For we Jews have a lot of experience being a marginalized, ridiculed minority. The advantage we Jews have is that we are old-timers at being a minority, whereas you Christians are newcomers to this condition." What now follows is some of the sympathetic advice I gave these Evangelical students, or what I might have given them had there been more time to do so.

Many Christians today are virtually traumatized by two interrelated facts. One, even though a majority of Americans (especially in the United States, but also in Canada) still identify as Christians, the fact is that in the three most powerful culture-forming institutions today—the universities, the media, and the courts—a committed Christian (maybe any Christian) is *now* a member of a definite, vulnerable minority. And Christians are a

1. In my inaugural lecture as the Shiff Chair in Jewish Studies at the University of Toronto, delivered on September 30, 1997, I dealt with the question of how somebody like myself, a rabbi who is an openly committed adherent of the Jewish tradition, could in good faith teach his tradition in a secular academic environment like that of the University of Toronto (the second oldest explicitly secular university in Canada) or that of the University of Virginia, which are places where there is great suspicion of any such religious commitment. The lecture itself, "The Jewish Ethical Tradition in the Modern University," was subsequently published in the *Journal of Education* (1998) 180:21–39, and in the *Journal of the Faculty of Religious Studies McGill University* (1998) 26:125–39.

2. This remark is quoted in Joseph I. Ellis, *American Sphinx: The Character of Thomas Jefferson* (New York: Knopf, 1997), 283.

minority who are highly suspect and regularly insulted. Not only is this a new experience of Christians for which you have little preparation, it is also your experience of a great loss, namely, your losing your majority status in America. Not so long ago, a majority of Americans were Protestant Christians. In fact, the ideal American of my youth (in the United States of the 1940s and 1950s) was a white Protestant Christian male, even though the United States has no "establishment of religion" (in the words of the first article of the Bill of Rights, appended to the US Constitution). Even if an American was not white, not a Protestant Christian, and not male, that American was expected—popularly if not officially—to model himself or herself on that ideal American nonetheless. After all, not to do so might suggest to one's fellow citizens in mid-twentieth-century America that he or she was a "Godless Communist."

Almost all of what had been "Christian America" is now gone, and the loss of that majority status is understandably painful for many Christians. However, those so pained often assume (whether consciously or not) that being *a* minority is a comedown from having formerly been *the* majority, especially when the new majority is either indifferent or actually hostile to them. For them, being the majority is good; being a minority is bad (especially when they were the majority until quite recently). There are also many Christians who simply acknowledge this reality and unhappily accept it as inevitable, assuming that they are simply on the wrong side of history (as they are often told by those who rejoice in their comedown), having no choice but to swallow this bitter pill. Yet there are other Christians who, while acknowledging that they are now a minority among an indifferent or hostile majority, do not accept this new fact as inevitable and irreversible. As my late lamented friend, Richard John Neuhaus, used to say to his followers and sympathizers, "We're going to turn this thing around!"[3] For Christians of this type, being a minority is something to be acknowledged in order *not* to accept it, but rather to resist it and thereby restore the *status quo ante.* Although, being very self-consciously American, these Christians are not calling for the restoration of European style "Christendom" along the lines of an *ancien régime.* The restoration they seek is a decidedly reformed, democratic, American one.

Now to both of these Christian reactions to their new minority status, Jews like me can empathize, in the sense of projecting ourselves into their

3. For the most important statement of his political and social philosophy, see *The Naked Public Square* (Grand Rapids: Eerdmans, 1984).

situation in order to understand it—but to understand it as an outsider. Even though there have been a few Jews in history who have aspired for the Jewish people to be a world majority, the overwhelming number of Jews have had no such aspirations. (Modern Jews who have had such aspirations are usually those who have seen the world-dominating program of Marxist Socialism, however inchoately, to somehow or other be what Judaism is all about, even though Marxists have been the explicit enemies of both Judaism and the singularity of the Jewish people.) Never having been the majority, though, certainly not in America, we Jews cannot offer sympathy—that is, *sympathein* or "feeling-with"—to Christians about the loss of a historical situation that has never been ours. We can only empathize with those Christians who fatally accept being a vulnerable minority in the sense of saying, "yes, we do know how you feel because of our long minority experience." Nevertheless, we Jews have no experience from which we can even empathize with those Christians who want to *restore* Christian majority status, both culturally and politically, as a desideratum. In fact, when some of us have been involved with Christians of this kind in what have been called the "Culture Wars," we have been able to do so when their agenda is largely an agenda based on natural law (i.e., universally valid moral law), which by definition is not derived from Christian—or Jewish—theology, even when it has been theologically nurtured by these Western religious traditions.[4]

Being a Minority: Good or Bad?

However, there is a position that can be taken by Christians, which, I think Jews like myself can truly sympathize with. That position truthfully acknowledges the new minority status of Christians, while not accepting this new status as a bad fate to be overcome by becoming the majority again. Instead, this third position not only accepts being a minority as a fact—that is, what *has been done* to Christians by forces beyond their control—but it simultaneously accepts this fact as something to be affirmed and for which Christians *should act* accordingly. Thus one not only accepts the fact of being a minority, one affirms in good faith that *to be a minority* is a good thing to be pursued. (I might add at this point that although Jews comprise and want to comprise the majority in the State of Israel, Jews still recognize that

4. See Anver Emon et al., *Natural Law: A Jewish, Christian, and Islamic Trialogue* (Oxford: Oxford University Press, 2014).

we are a small people in the larger world; and we have no agenda to Judaize the whole world, thus making ourselves the majority of humankind.)

Christians, like Jews, though, cannot be satisfied with merely defining themselves negatively against the culture-forming majority, for such essentially negative self-identification on the part of a minority needs that majority more than that majority needs them. That is, a minority needs the threatening majority as a negative "other" *against* whom it must perpetually struggle as the fundamental assertion of its identity, both to itself and to the world. Conversely, to be a minority, even among an indifferent and frequently hostile majority, is something to be pursued positively. To be sure, a minority must be ever vigilant in the face of the majority who surround them; it cannot try to be indifferent to them without dangerous consequences. The sectarian option of maximal isolation from the majority (like that of the Amish as Christians and the Hasidim as Jews) takes away from a minority its political independence, thereby giving the majority greater power over them because of their own self-marginalization. That is why a minority has to be politically proactive, not only on issues of its own particular self-interest like tax exemptions for religious institutions, but even more so on issues of public morality like abortion, euthanasia, and racial discrimination that affect the lives of all citizens, themselves included. (On these issues, political and theological positions cannot be totally separated.) On both counts, being proactive is necessary for the political and economic survival of the minority community.[5] Yet, in the end, even being proactive politically is still an essentially negative task and goal insofar as it is basically defensive. It is still doing what is necessary, but not what is desirable, per se. As Esther told Mordecai when their persecuted minority community was under threat, "relief and deliverance will arise for the Jews from another place" (Esth 4:14).[6] Politics won't provide Jews or Christians with their positive task and goal; only theology can do that.

In order to reach a point of theological commonality, however, the political reflection above had to be done first; for without it we would be engaging in dialogue that is oblivious to the social world in which we are now living. Without this prior political reflection, our truly sympathetic

5. See David Novak, *In Defense of Religious Liberty* (Wilmington, DE: ISI, 2009), 3–28.

6. All translations, unless otherwise noted, are by the author. The rabbinic texts cited in this essay, though no doubt unfamiliar to almost all of my readers, are cited nonetheless, if for no other reason than to show that the claims made in this essay, arguable to be sure, are still based on considerable precedent in the Jewish tradition.

dialogue would be conducted in an historical vacuum, having little connection to our joint situation in this humanly constructed social world. Even though we are not "of the world" in the sense that we do not look to the world for "our help" (Ps 121:1–2), we are still "in the world" in the sense that whatever help comes to us from sources above the world can only be intelligently accepted when we know where we are in this world here and now, i.e., for the time being.[7] Among other things, that means we do not flee the world.[8] That is our lot and our task until God brings the world-beyond (i.e., beyond the temporal horizon of this world) as "the new heaven and new earth" (Isa 66:22), which are to be brought "for those who wait for Him" (Isa 64:3).[9]

Minority Theology

With Evangelical Christians (whether Catholic or Protestant), a traditional Jew like myself can truly sympathize, i.e., when there is a place for us to feel or experience our vulnerable minorityness and begin to appreciate it as something good and not something bad, and to act accordingly. That immovable, ever-present place is Scripture, more specifically that Scripture which you Christians call the *Old Testament* and which we Jews call the *Written Torah*, and which we share as "the word of our God that endures forever" (Isa 40:8). In fact, our greatest Jewish theologian, Maimonides, already in the twelfth century taught that Jews may, perhaps should, study Torah with Christians, because faithful Christians like faithful Jews

---

7. When Jesus said he and his disciples are "not of or from the world' (*ek tou kosmou*), but that he and his disciples "are sent into the world" (*eis ton kosmon*) in John 17:15, 18, he was uttering sound Jewish doctrine. So too in John 18:36–37, when Jesus said to Pontius Pilate: "my kingdom is not from this world" (*ek tou kosmou*), but that he "came into the world" (*eis ton kosmon*), he was uttering sound Jewish doctrine. Thus the ancient rabbis taught that the Torah is "from God" (*min ha-shamayim*), and it is to be learned for "the sake of God's kingdom" (*le-shem shamayim*), though it functions in this world, i.e., here on earth and "not in heaven" (*lo ba-shamayim*). See *Mishnah*: Sanhedrin 10.1, and Avot 2.12; *Babylonian Talmud*: Baba Metsia 59b re Deut 30:12.

8. Cf. Plato, *Theatetus*, 176A-B.

9. I have translated *olam ha-ba* (literally, "the coming world") as the "world-beyond" (i.e., beyond the temporal horizon of this world, which we humans ordinarily experience). It is virtually identical with the rabbinic term *l`atid la-vo* (literally, "the future-yet-to-come"), which could be translated as the "radical future" as distinct from the imminent or predictable future (*ha-nolad*; literally "what can be expected to be born"). See *Babylonian Talmud*: Avodah Zarah 3b; *Mishnah*: Avot 2.13.

unambivalently accept the Torah as perfect revelation from God.[10] Now, truth be told, Maimonides saw Christians as having veered from Judaism due to their incorrect interpretation of some scriptural teachings; yet this difference presupposes prior commonality, and that commonality—too often obscured in the past—is our concern here and now for very pressing reasons.

Furthermore, our common acceptance of the same body of revelation—the Hebrew Scriptures—is because both Jews and Christians consider themselves to be *Israel*, the people God elects for a covenantal relationship through the revelation of God's Torah to them to be their communal constitution. Of course, there are Christians whom we call "supersessionists" who claim that the Christian church is now the only true Israel, and that the Jewish people have had their covenantal status removed from them by God in favor of the church (i.e., the Jews have been be replaced by the church in the covenant). And there are Jews who claim that when the Christians ceased to be a Jewish sect and separated themselves from the Jewish people, they thereby became just another gentile people in this world and even more so in the world-beyond (*olam ha-ba*).[11] This kind of Christian and this kind of Jew might have some political commonality, now being two minorities (among a number of other minorities) in the same society, but they are theologically indifferent if not antagonistic to one another.

On the other hand, though, there are Jews who do not deny Christian claims to be Israel (i.e., as long as Christians do not regard the church to have displaced the Jewish people in the House of Israel with themselves). Now it is taught that "all Israel have a portion in the world-beyond." Even though in this world, at best Christians (as well as Muslims) can only be taken to be monotheists living under a divine revealed law, yet by their full acceptance of the Mosaic Torah, faithful Christians can be seen as full members, along with faithful Jews, of what might be termed "eschatological Israel" (i.e., Israel in the world-beyond).[12] And Christians who see themselves as "the

10. For Maimonides's actual statement, see David Novak, *Jewish-Christian Dialogue: A Jewish Justification* (New York: Oxford University Press, 1989), 64–67.

11. *Tosefta*: Sanhedrin 13.2, and *Babylonian Talmud*: Sanhedrin 105a re Ps 9:18 (the opinion of Rabbi Eliezer).

12. *Mishnah*: Sanhedrin 10.1 re Isa 60:21; *Tosefta*: Sanhedrin 13.2; and *Babylonian Talmud*: Sanhedrin 105a re Ps 9:18 (the opinion of Rabbi Joshua); Maimonides, *Mishneh Torah*: Kings 8:11. Moreover, it should be noted that while in this world, being Jewish is a matter of indelible birth (or equally indelible rebirth through conversion; *Babylonian Talmud*: Sanhedrin 44a re Josh 7:11), being a participant in the world-beyond is denied

branch grafted unto the tree" (Rom 11:16–19) can surely accept this Jewish
teaching and thus respect the respective independence of the church from
the Jewish people and the Jewish people from the church in this world, even
though they do not extend this separation to the world-beyond. Moreover,
Maimonides taught that the world-beyond is really God's eternal kingdom
within which this world is a temporal island, and which humans can properly participate in when keeping the commandments God has provided for
us to be connected to it here and now, however incompletely.[13] Hence our
connection to that "other" world is not only a matter of belief about what
transcends us, but it is a matter of actual praxis in the present as well.[14] (I
think this view of the world-beyond as the world that transcends us, but
which we do not transcend, protects us from thinking of that world as some
sort of future utopia to which we are only connected by what seem to be
fantasies rather than by real experience.)

The separation of our two communities from each other in this world
(*ha`olam ha-zeh*) is necessary because of our different connections to the
world-beyond as two different eschatologically oriented communities with
their different traditions. Our Jewish connection to the world-beyond
is the Written Torah plus the Oral Torah, what later came to be known
as "Rabbinic" or "Talmudic" Judaism. Your Christian connection to the
world-beyond is Jesus as the Christ, who based all his claims on the Written
Torah (Matt 5:17–19). We Jews live our connection to that world through
the positive commandments of the Torah (such as the Sabbath and festivals
like Passover) as rabbinically interpreted. You Christians live your connection to that world through the sacraments as interpreted by the church (as
the body of Christ). This great difference (what the French would call *la
différence même*) is much too great to be overcome by either of us in this
world. In fact, it could only be overcome by one of us conquering the other
or by the minority voluntarily assimilating into the majority. But that is
an option neither of us should entertain, especially because of our mutual
experience of now being the objects of conquest or seduction by modern
Post-Enlightenment Secularism, either overtly or more covertly by the type

---

to those who do not actively affirm (or who at least do not explicitly deny) three cardinal
Jewish dogmas: the existence of God, the revelation of the Torah, and the resurrection of
the dead (*Mishnah*: Sanhedrin 10.1).

13. *Mishneh Torah*: Repentance, 8.8.

14. *Babylonian Talmud*: Berakhot 4a re Ps 27:13–14.

of ongoing political and cultural marginalization we examined at the beginning of this essay.

The Doctrine of Election

One of the great challenges for scriptural interpretation is to determine whether a particular passage is descriptive or prescriptive, that is, is it telling us what *is* or what *ought to be*? Obviously, there are passages that couldn't be anything but prescriptive, for example, "Everything the Lord is commanding [*tsivah*] you through Moses, which the Lord commands henceforth for [all] your generations" (Num 15:23). But there are other passages that are not explicitly prescriptive. Whenever possible, though, the ancient rabbis tried to at least derive something normative, such as a counsel or evaluation from them. After all, the word "Torah" itself means "normative instruction." So, let us try to follow suit when dealing with a scriptural passage that speaks of the minority status of the people Israel. "Not because of your being more numerous than all the other peoples does the Lord desire you and choose you, for you are the least numerous [*ha-me`at*] of all the peoples" (Deut 7:7). The key to understanding the normative meaning of this passage hinges on the word *ki*, translated here as "for." Now this word most often introduces a clause of a sentence as the reason or purpose of what is stated either before or after it in the sentence. As such, the words "for [*ki*] you are the least numerous of all the peoples" give the reason *why* God chooses the people Israel. And, by clear implication, this is the reason *why* God didn't choose any of the other peoples, all of whom seem to be "more numerous" than Israel.[15] This passage is normative in the sense of being an example of God's exercise of wise autonomy (i.e., God's commanding Godself, deliberately planning to do something for a good reason).[16] As such, the human choice to actively affirm one's being

15. LXX's translation of the Hebrew *lo me-rubbekhem* as *oukh hoti polyplētheite* could plausibly be translated as "because you are not the majority." Both the Hebrew and the Greek speak of "you" in the second-person plural.

16. Only God is autonomous in the sense of alone being able to plan to do something unconditionally (i.e., being able to create *ex nihilo* the options from which God then chooses to do one rather than the others). Human creatures, conversely, have freedom of choice (see Deut 30:19) in the sense of being able to choose, but only to select from options *already* present in the world (see Eccl 1:10). It was Immanuel Kant (in many ways the patron saint of modern philosophical secularism) who basically removed autonomy from God and transferred it to human moral agents. For the most powerful critique

chosen by God to be a member of this minority people, that itself is an act of *imitatio Dei*. Thus when Joshua admonished the people Israel, "you have chosen [*behartem lakhem*] the Lord to serve Him" (Josh 24:22), he was telling the people to actively confirm God's choice of them, and to be what God chooses them to be.

Now it is a principle of rabbinic exegesis that one may "infer the positive from the negative."[17] In our passage, we might see why God didn't choose those other peoples, and then infer the obverse, which is why God does choose Israel. That might be seen in the words usually translated as "because of your being more numerous," but which could be translated as "because of your larger numbers (*me-rubbekhem*)," i.e., your greater population. In other words, being more numerous than others—which the people Israel clearly are not—is the reason why God did not choose any of the more numerous peoples. Perhaps the words "*your* numerousness" indicate that a numerous people is more likely to attribute their strength of numbers to themselves. For strength of numbers is worldly power, the type of power that so easily tempts a people to believe that they have chosen themselves rather than being chosen by God. Indeed, Israel is warned not to be a people who proclaim "my strength and the power of my hand have accomplished all this success [*ha-hayil*]" (Deut 8:17). The difference is that a people who choose themselves usually do so in order to make conquest their task and purpose in the world, with God being on their side as some sort of cosmic facilitator (*Gott mit uns,* in the words of the World War I German slogan). But a people truly aware of their being chosen by God begin to understand that their task and purpose is to be God's "portion" in the world (Deut 4:20). And they can only do this by living the life of covenantal intimacy with God as specified by the Torah. The members of a small people, indeed a very small people, are much less likely to be seduced into the pursuit of worldly conquest than are the members of a very large, numerous people.

In the end, though, isn't this a negative reason insofar as we are only told why God didn't choose any other people, but not why God does choose Israel? However, if God were to tell Israel why he chooses them, that revelation could only be because of some property Israel *has* or something very righteous Israel *has done*, and for this righteousness Israel's election into

---

(theological or otherwise) of Kant on autonomy, see Karl Barth, *Church Dogmatics*, 2/2, trans. G. W. Bromiley et al. (Edinburgh: T. and T. Clark, 1957), 650–66.

17. *Babylonian Talmud*: Nedarim 11a.

the covenant with God is their just reward, their payment for past services rendered. Yet the Torah warns the people that they shouldn't arrogantly believe their election by God is "due to your righteousness" (Deut 9:5). For self-righteousness is self-justification (*tsedaqah*). Certainly, "the righteous person [*tsaddiq*] who lives in his faith" (Hab 2:4) does not live through his or her faith as self-justifying action; instead, he or she lives in the life of the object of their faith, who is God.[18]

To assume that God's choice is capricious, without a good reason, would be to indict God as being inferior to a wise human ruler and lawgiver, and thus hardly the One whom any wise person would or could imitate.[19] So it seems better to surmise that God knows something Israel *has* making her worthy of election, but which God has chosen not to reveal, lest the people Israel become self-righteous. Or maybe God's reason is prospective (i.e., an anticipation of the special role Israel *will* play in God's redemption of the world). But that redemption is God's project, not Israel's. Hence the people Israel's task in this world is to live faithfully according to the Torah, but to be fully aware and to fully accept that their future role in God's eschatological plan is by no means their lot here and now. "The secrets are the Lord our God's, but the things revealed [*ve-ha-niglot*] are for us and our children to do [*la'asot*] for the time-being [*ad olam*]: all the words of this Torah" (Deut 29:28).[20] Furthermore, "My plans [*mahshevotai*] are not your

18. According to one opinion in *Babylonian Talmud*: Makkot 24a, this is considered to be the single most succinct statement of what the Torah's message is. The view that one's faith is itself meritorious is a Jewish view that Paul made famous (Rom 4:3 and Gal 3:5–6 re Gen 15:6). For a similar post-Christian Jewish view, see the comment of the eleventh-century French-Jewish exegete Rashi on Genesis 15:6 in *Pentateuch with Rashi's Commentary*, trans. M. Rosenbaum and A. M. Silverman (London: Shapiro, Vallentine, 1946), 1:60. The view that it is Abraham who confirms the righteousness of God, rather than vice-versa, is the view of the thirteenth-century Spanish-Jewish theologian Nahmanides in his comment on Genesis 15:6. See David Novak, *The Theology of Nahmanides Systematically Presented* (Chico, CA: Scholars, 1992), 42. Both Rashi and Nahmanides lived in Christian societies and they were quite familiar with Christian theology. They also had contact with contemporary Christian theologians (all of which might not have been disputational).

19. See Maimonides, *Guide of the Perplexed*, 3.26 re Deut 32:47, trans. S. Pines (Chicago: University of Chicago Press, 1963), 506–7, and 3.54 re Jer 9:23, 637–38.

20. Here I have followed the German translation of Martin Buber and Franz Rosenzweig: *für Weltzeit* in *Die Fünf Bücher der Weisung* (Cologne: Jakob Hegner, 1954), 554. It would seem that for the third-century rabbi, Yohanan bar Nappaha (a contemporary of Origen in Roman Palestine) and for Paul, these divine "secrets" might be revealed in the world-beyond, which is beyond the horizon of "world-time" (*Weltzeit*). See *Babylonian Talmud*: Berakhot 34b re Isa 64:3, and 1 Cor 2:9 re Isa 64:3.

plans, and your ways are not Mine, says the Lord. For as the heavens are higher than the earth, so are My ways higher than your ways and my plans than yours" (Isa 55:8–9).

A Light of the Nations

Heretofore, two propositions have been set forth about how a minority religious community—especially, Jewish or Christian—is to be related to the larger majority community occupying the same society. The first proposition is that a religious minority ought not aspire to majority status and strive to attain it by their own human devices. The second proposition is that a religious minority should concentrate their efforts on developing and deepening the covenantal life they share with God.[21] As such, this kind of community should primarily look inward, not outward. Nevertheless, the question remains: How can a minority community see being related to the majority in a positive way?

Perhaps a minority religious community could attempt to bring the majority around to their religious stance by proselytizing them. That is by persuading the "gentile" or "pagan" majority to join the minority community by accepting its fundamental teachings as the highest truth available to humans in this world, and for the sake of their admission to the world-beyond. That would then turn the minority community, so augmented, into the majority community. The question that should concern us in this inquiry, especially, is whether such a proselytizing program requires accessing the political and cultural power of the majority to be effective. And if so, what protects the minority from being the tool of the majority to be either used or discarded? (Most of the "throne-altar" struggles in European history were struggles over whether the church was to be the handmaiden of the state or vice-versa.)

To deal with this question theologically, let us look at a key scriptural passage which, according to most modern Bible scholars, comes from the time when the Jewish people began to seek full proselytes.[22] That was the

21. The ancient Rabbis speak of the humans in this relationship as being "the partners of God in the work of creation" (*Babylonian Talmud*: Shabbat 119b re Gen 2:1). However, that partnership is mentioned in connection with the keeping of the Sabbath, which is considered to be an activity between God and Israel alone (*Babylonian Talmud*: Sanhedrin 58b re Gen 8:22).

22. For the distinction between a full proselyte (*ger tsedeq*) and a "sojourner" (*ger*), who the Rabbis called a "resident-alien" (*ger toshav*), see *Babylonian Talmud*: Baba Kama

time when the Judeans (*yehudim* or "Jews") returned to the land of Israel from Babylonian captivity in the middle of the fifth century BCE. (That is important to note because there is no explicit biblical evidence that there were full proselytes in the days of the First Temple, i.e., before 586 BCE.)

The verse reads: "I shall make you the light of the nations [*l'or goyyim*] in order that My salvation [*yeshu'ati*] might be unto the ends of the earth" (Isa 49:6). The question to be asked about this passage is: Just how does God's salvation (which seems to be the "light" the gentiles will see and be attracted to) reach the gentile nations?[23] Is this a prophecy that the people Israel will themselves bring the light "the Lord shines [*zarach*] on you" (Isa 60:1) to the gentiles, and then the gentiles they do reach will respond to Israel's proselytizing efforts by becoming full members of Israel by conversion? Or, is this prophesying that the gentiles will see the light God shines on Israel and they will become full members of Israel by conversion, but by their own initiative and not because of any efforts on Israel's part?[24] Therefore, it could be said that the first option advocates proselytizing for the sake of conversion, while the second option passively permits conversion, yet it does not advocate active proselytizing. Moreover, a second question to be asked here is: What is meant by the "light" (*or*) that is seen by both Israel and the gentiles and which attracts them?

The standard Christian answer to the two questions above can be stated as follows. No doubt, the New Testament advocates active proselytizing. Jesus' last words to his disciples are: "Therefore, go [*poreuthentes*] and

---

113b re Lev 25:47. For the doctrine that a full proselyte is "born again" by virtue of his or her conversion (*giyyur*), see *Babylonian Talmud*: Yevamot 32a and parallels. Cf. John 3:3–7.

23. See Psalm 27:1 for both "light" and "salvation" being attributed to God. For *goyyim* ("the nations") meaning what the rabbis called "the nations of the world" (*ummot ha'olam* as in *Sifra*: Aharei-Mot, ch. 13 re Lev 18:4, ed. Weiss, 86a), see Psalm 79:6. In rabbinic texts, *goyyim* came to mean individual gentiles (e.g., *Palestinian Talmud*: Bikkurim 1.4/64a re Gen 17:5). This is important to note here, since the gentiles who were converted to Judaism in the postexilic period came to be converted as individuals, not as whole groups. See *Palestinian Talmud*: Berakhot 2.8/5c re Song 6:2.

24. A thirteenth-century French rabbi (at a time when Jews were forbidden by the officially Christian state to accept gentile converts), commenting on a Talmudic passage that seems to be opposed to conversion at all, argued that this only meant converts who had been proselytized by Jews, or who had been converted too hastily, but not those who by their own initiative insisted on being converted to Judaism (*Babylonian Talmud*: Yevamot 109b, *Tosafot*, s.v. "ra'ah"). See, also, *Babylonian Talmud*: Kiddushin 70b–71a re Isa 14:1 and *Tosafot*, s.v. "qashim" (the opinion of Rabbi Abraham the Convert).

teach all the nations [*panta ta ethnē*], baptizing them, etc."²⁵ We also see the words of Isaiah 49:6 in the blessing Simeon gives to the infant Jesus in the Temple, saying to God, "For my eyes have seen Your salvation [*to sōtērion*], which You have set before [*prosōpon*] all the peoples: a light to be revealed [*eis apokalypsin*] to the nations, and the glory of Your people Israel."²⁶ Now the light to be revealed to the gentiles is the revelation of Jesus as the Savior (*sōtēr*). Yet, how are the gentile nations to see this light, especially since Jesus himself was not internationally known either in life or in death (and even his resurrection was only known to his immediate disciples)? It would seem that the only way they could see this light and be attracted to it/him is when Jesus's subsequent disciples themselves bring this light to the gentiles (i.e., when the disciples—now the church—*enlighten* the gentiles with the gospel).²⁷ Hence what is literally stated "as a light *of* the nations" (*l'or goyyim*) now in effect becomes "a light *to* the nations" (*or la-goyyim*), i.e., *the light to be brought to the whole world.*²⁸

However, the text of Isaiah 49:6 can be read according to the second option above, and this is generally how Jews—especially after the rise of Christianity—have read this text. That is, the text can be interpreted to mean that God's shining his light on Israel will make a profound impression on the gentiles. Because of their awareness of what God has done for and with Israel, "nations [*goyyim*] will walk *to* *y*our light [*l'orekh*]" (Isa 60:3), which is the light God shines on Israel. It is God's action that brings gentiles to the light God has shone on Israel. That is not because the people Israel see themselves to be God's messengers to the gentiles. In fact, such an assumption could well turn into the presumption that the messengers are

25. Matthew 28:19.

26. Luke 2:30–32.

27. This comes out when Jesus tells his disciples "you are the light of the world [*tou kosmou*]," which "cannot be hid [*krybēnai*] (Matt 5:14, i.e., it is "revealed" so that "your light shine [*lampsatō*] before [*emprosthen*] men" [5:16]). See Mark 4:21–22. It is what their light "makes manifest" (*eis phaneron*—Luke 8:17), which is Jesus' messiahhood.

28. Precedence for this, I think, comes from LXX (which is frequently the Greek version of the Hebrew Scriptures invoked in the New Testament), both on Isaiah 49:6 and 42:6 where the text says *l'or goyyim*. LXX states *eis phōs ethnōn*. This could well mean that the Hebrew text, as if written *le-ha'ir goyyim*, viz., "to enlighten the gentiles." This also reflects the fact that active proselytizing seems to have been much more prevalent in Hellenistic Judaism than it was in later rabbinic Judaism (see *supra*, n. 24). In earlier Pharisaic Judaism, though, we have the statement of the first-century sage, Hillel the Elder, "love humankind [*ha-beriyot*] and draw them near to the Torah" (*Mishnah*: Avot 1.12; see, also *Babylonian Talmud*: Shabbat 31a).

as important as the message, and that they are even as important as the One who is the Subject and Sender of the message. And, in this interpretation of "a light of the gentiles," what exactly is this *light*? The answer to this question depends on *when* one thinks this light shines. Is it when this light *will* shine then, or is it when this light *is* shining now?

On the one hand, if one holds that this light will shine in the radical, eschatological *future*, then clearly the light here is the appearance of the Messiah, when it will be said, "The people who walk in darkness have seen a great light" (Isa 9:1). That "great light" is the real appearance of the Messiah, when "authority will be on his shoulders . . . [when there will be] unlimited peace [*u-le-shalom*] on David's throne and kingship" (Isa 9:5–6). It is to this Messiah-yet-to-come that "many peoples [*ammim rabbim*] will come" (Isa 2:3) to be instructed in the law of God.[29] It seems that the gentiles will come of their own accord, and that they will come as communities, not as random individuals. That makes sense inasmuch as the Messiah is primarily a king (*melekh*), the ruler of a kingdom (*mamlakhah*), and, as such, he is most likely to deal officially with others politically (i.e., with a public rather than nonpolitically with private persons).

On the other hand, if one holds that this light is shining now, then clearly the light is not the appearance of the Messiah in this world. For both Jews and Christians, the Messiah is not to be found in this world as it is here and now. For Jews, the Messiah will first come in a future radically different from the present. For Christians, the Messiah will come again similarly. So, what is the light here that attracts both Israel, who continue to see the light already shown to them in the past, and the gentiles who are now beginning to see it? It would seem that light is the Torah that God has revealed to Israel, and which Israel is not to keep to themselves. "Your word is a lamp to my feet and light [*v'or*] to my path" (Ps 119:105).[30] This is the light to which the gentiles will be attracted to; and already in the Hellenistic Age, that attraction could be easily acted upon, because Jews in the Hellenistic world (like in Egypt, Syria, and Asia Minor) were reading the Torah in the Greek of the Septuagint in their synagogues, and unlike the Jerusalem Temple, gentiles were free to enter the main area of the synagogue where the Torah

29. The notion that the law of God will be considerably different in the messianic era as Christians taught (Matt 12:8) is entertained by some of the Rabbis (e.g., *Tosefta*: Berakhot 1.10 re Jer 23:7). For further discussion of this complex issue, see David Novak, "Law and Eschatology: A Jewish-Christian Intersection," *Talking with Christians: Musings of a Jewish Theologian* (Grand Rapids: Eerdmans, 2005), 46–66.

30. Along these lines, see *Babylonian Talmud*: Sotah 35b re Deut 27:8.

was read and expounded and worship was conducted. Thus they were exposed to Judaism in both word and deed (i.e., both from what the Jews said from the Torah and how they acted accordingly to the Torah.[31] Moreover, they were to be attracted for religious rather than for political reasons).[32]

So, when it is prescribed in the Talmud (during the time of overbearing Roman rule in Palestine) just what to tell somebody coming to convert, the first thing he or she is to be told is how politically impotent and vulnerable the Jewish people are now. That is to discourage anybody naïve enough to be converted for political reasons. And the next thing they are to be told is specifically Jewish religious obligations, and then the beneficial otherworldly consequences for those Jews who keep these commandments in this dangerous world.[33] Indeed, how different from this is it when Jesus tells Satan "be gone" when Satan him offers worldly power?[34] Or, how different from this is it when Jesus tells Pontius Pilate (who is told he is a political threat), "my kingdom is not from [ek] this world?"[35] To be sure that does not mean that Jews or Christians should eschew political and economic independence wherever they happen to live in this world. Nevertheless, neither Jews nor Christians should confuse the worldly power they need with the kingdom of God they desire. Caesar is due what Caesar deserves, but nothing more or less.[36]

---

31. Along these lines, the lights kindled on Hanukkah are meant to proclaim to all (*pirsumei nisa*), not the military-political victory of the Maccabees, but rather the religiously significant event of the cleansing of the Temple of the pagan cult introduced there by the Hellenistic Syrians and their Jewish followers, epitomized by the rekindling of the *menorah* there (*Babylonian Talmud*: Yevamot 21b and 24b; Arakhin 10b). It is sad to note that it was often the case in medieval Christian societies that it was dangerous for Jews to publicize the miracle, and they had to keep the Hanukkah lights hidden behind the closed doors of their homes (Rabbi Moses Isserles's note on Rabbi Joseph Karo, *Shulhan Arukh*: Orah Hayyim, 671.7). Happily, in democracies like ours, where Jews can practice Judaism openly, members of the *Chabad* community have revived the ancient practice of lighting Hanukkah lights in many public places in North America.

32. In fact, there was great suspicion of those who in the past had converted due to what seem to have been political motives, i.e., to be close to the center of Jewish political power (*Babylonian Talmud*: Yevamot 24b).

33. *Babylonian Talmud*: Yevamot 47a-b re Ruth 1:16–17.

34. Matthew 4:10.

35. John 18:36.

36. See Matthew 22:21. For arguments against both Jewish political quietism and Jewish nationalistic messianism in favor of a theologically cogent Zionism that is neither (which Christians as well as Jews can appreciate), see David Novak, *Zionism and Judaism: A New Theory* (Cambridge: Cambridge University Press, 2015), 225–49. There

To Proselytize or Not to Proselytize?

We have seen above that proselytizing, which is the active recruitment of gentiles into the covenanted community, needs to be wary of being attached to the majority and its program of political domination of this minority and all other minorities along with it. Yet, isn't this a problem for Christians who do actively proselytize rather than for Jews who do not actively proselytize? However, the fact that Jews do not seem to proselytize does not mean that the Jewish tradition actually forbids Jews from doing so. It is the experience of Jews rather than the Jewish tradition that has made proselytizing a program the vast majority of Jews do not want and have not wanted for almost two millennia. Nevertheless, what can you Christians learn from the seemingly universal Jewish aversion to proselytizing?

There are three reasons for this longtime Jewish aversion to proselytizing. One, until the rise of modern, secular nation-states in the late eighteenth century, Jews were forbidden by the Christians states, in which they lived as a tolerated yet vulnerable minority, to convert non-Jews to Judaism on the pain of death. Two, even when this kind of religious imperialism was gone officially, there was still the social pressure for Jews to convert to the religion of the Christian majority rather than even attempting to bring non-Jews (whether Christian or not) into the Jewish people as converts. Because of these social pressures, many Jews, especially in Western Europe, converted to Christianity; and many of them were probably more politically than religiously motivated. As such, those Jews who remained faithful to the Torah and Jewish tradition barely had enough energy to persuade their fellow Jews to remain Jewish and thus retain them for Judaism. Moreover, there was very little interest among non-Jews to become Jews themselves (aside from a few who had to do so in order to marry Jews who still insisted on officially Jewish spouses). Three, most Jews have had the unpleasant experience of being the objects of Christian proselytizing efforts. As the first century sage Hillel the Elder famously taught, "what is hateful to you, do not you to somebody else."[37]

While the first reason for the consistent Jewish aversion to proselytizing is no longer valid, the second and third reasons are still valid; and Christians can learn something important from them.

(197–224), I also argue for the rights of non-Jewish minorities in a majority Jewish state constituted according to the Torah.

37. *Babylonian Talmud*: Shabbat 31a.

Christian efforts at active proselytizing have been their strongest when Christians have been the overwhelming majority in a society, and when Christians have had the power of the state on their side. The task most Christians saw for themselves then was to close the gap they perceived between being the majority of the citizenry and being the total citizenry. That was to be done by converting the minority who were still holdouts or driving them away altogether (as was done to the Jewish and Muslim minorities in Spain in 1492 when the *Reconquista* or re-Christianization of Spain had been finally completed). And this was also done when in the Christian conquests of non-European societies (such as those in the Western Hemisphere), the *conquistadores* brought the missionaries along with them. But that is no longer the case anywhere in the world today, so there is no need for Jews or any other group of non-Jews to worry about the first reason for their historical aversion to proselytizing. We Jews are no longer the vulnerable objects of this kind of proselytizing.

The second reason for Jewish aversion to ourselves being proselytizers is because we have enough of a problem retaining our own people within the covenantal fold, and also bringing those Jews who have strayed from the fold into other folds or no fold back home.[38] That does not mean we Jews ignore gentiles who want to convert to Judaism; we don't. It is just that we have more pressing concerns, and we must therefore understand our priorities. Now it seems to me that you Christians have a very similar problem. Considering the considerable drop in the numbers of Americans who still call themselves "Christians," as well as the drop in attendance at the churches of most of the Christian denominations, let it not be said about you, "my own vineyard I did not keep" (Song 1:6). Now I am not telling you to abandon what you consider to be your essential Christian task to preach the gospel to the whole world. That you could not do in good faith. I am only suggesting that proselytizing might no longer be your major priority.

The third reason for Jewish aversion to proselytizing is that most of us do not want to do what we did not want others to do to us. This kind of proselytizing almost always told us what we were doing as faithful Jews is bad, or that we Jews need to be told how much better somebody else's religion is for us, or that we Jews are potential Christians inasmuch as Christianity is the true fulfillment of our Judaism. But something has happened in the last fifty years or so that has made all three of these kinds of

38. See David Novak, *The Election of Israel: The Idea of the Chosen People* (Cambridge: Cambridge University Press, 1995), 189–99.

proselytization of Jews less prevalent and less militant than they had been even in the very recent past. That new factor is Jewish-Christian dialogue. For dialogue presupposes an even playing field between the parties in the dialogue. Any attempt on the part of either party to minimize, conquer, or assimilate one party into the other will surely kill an authentic dialogue even before it gets off the ground. Now, from my virtually lifelong involvement in Jewish-Christian dialogue, I have found that the overwhelming number of my Christian dialogue partners have not so much as abandoned any proselytizing efforts in general (which would actually be rather untrue to Christian tradition and thus suspect) as they have carefully bracketed it. (And their proselytizing efforts are generally directed, without specifically targeting Jews.) They believe they can do both separately and without ultimate contradiction. And even though there are some of my fellow Jews who call me naïve for thinking this dialogical interest is anything but an elaborate ruse for covert proselytizing, my experience with both Catholic and Protestant dialogue partners tells me otherwise.[39]

In conclusion, I hope that this dialogue can be an instantiation of the words of Malachi, the last of the prophets quoted in Scripture, namely, "Those who fear the Lord, each speaking to his neighbor" (Mal 3:16). And being minorities who recognize this fact and who see in it an opportunity gives us both much to talk about and much to do with each other in the world we share together with other minorities. Yet we two, Christians and Jews, are the two minorities who have the most in common theologically. That is an old truth, yet one only recently rediscovered. Against the backdrop of our two-thousand-year history of frequently painful interrelation in the world, this new situation is in the words of the poet Robert Frost, "the road less traveled by, and that has made all the difference."[40]

---

39. That experience led three other Jewish scholars and myself in 2000 to publish *Dabru Emet: A Jewish Statement on Christians and Christianity* (www.jcrelations.net/Dabru_Emet), which was signed by over 200 rabbis and Jewish leaders, and which has been translated into at least eight languages. It also led to the publication of the companion volume, *Christianity in Jewish Terms*, ed. Tikva Frymer-Kensky *et al.* (Boulder, CO: Westview, 2000).

40. "The Road Not Taken," in *Seven Centuries of Verse: English and American*, 2nd rev. edn., ed. A. J. M. Smith (New York: Scribner, 1957), 589.

4

A Tree Planted by Streams of Water: Scriptural Lessons on Hope

Kathryn Schifferdecker

THE THEME OF THIS volume, "The Emerging Christian Minority," came home to me in a concrete way recently as I was preparing this essay. I was driving to work, listening to National Public Radio, when the "Friday Round Table" began. The "Friday Round Table" is a local Twin Cities radio call-in show, hosted by a woman named Kerri Miller. This particular segment was on "the books we pretend to read," that is, books that we lie about having read. Have you read *A Tale of Two Cities*, *Moby Dick*, *War and Peace*? Yes, of course, I've read them all. Who hasn't?

One guest admitted that the book that he lies most often about reading is the Bible. He went on to explain that he belonged to an Awana group as a child. Awana (as I'm sure most of you know) is an evangelical Christian education program for children. He had as a child earned merit badges in this group for memorizing Scripture passages, but the only one he could remember now, he said, was John 3:16, and that one only because he watched football games.

"John 3:16?" said the host, "I don't know that one. And what does it have to do with football games?"

Now, it must be emphasized that this was a National Public Radio host, who, if stereotypes hold true, likely neither reads the Bible nor watches football games. Still, being a Christian and a professor of Bible, I was aghast. Really? You don't know what John 3:16 is? The guest, stumbling quite a bit, quoted the verse from the King James Version. "For God so loved the world that he gave his only begotten Son, that whosoever believeth in him should not perish, but have everlasting life."

And then the host asked, "I still don't understand. Why would people hold that up at a football game?" And the guest responded, "I have *no* idea." Then the interview turned to other subjects.

The emerging Christian minority, indeed. I realize this is a very small incident, but a telling one. We who do know John 3:16 and understand why someone would hold it up at a football game, even if we wouldn't do so ourselves, are apparently becoming an oddity in our society. And the realization of this situation can be a very unnerving experience, especially for those of us whose vocations have to do with proclaiming the gospel of Jesus Christ and teaching others to do the same.

Like a Tree

I was asked to write about hope, particularly scriptural lessons on hope. There are many places one can go to in Scripture to talk about hope, of course, and I will not begin to touch on all of them, but I want to begin with a passage that I particularly love, one that provides the image for my title.

A tree planted by streams of water. It is with this beautiful image that the book of Psalms begins. Listen to the first few verses of Psalm 1:

> Happy the one who does not walk in the counsel of the wicked,
> who does not stand in the way of sinners,
> who does not sit in the seat of scoffers.
> But in the torah of the LORD is his delight
> and on his *torah* he meditates day and night.
> That one is like a tree planted by streams of water,
> which yields fruit in its season,
> and its leaves do not wither.
> In all that he does, he prospers. (Ps 1:1–3)[1]

The psalmist draws a stark contrast in this psalm between two different paths. One can walk with the wicked and stand with scoffers and sit in the company of mockers. Many people do so. The scoffers and the mockers

---

1. Author's translation. All other Scripture quotations are from the NRSV unless otherwise noted.

are, after all, witty, sophisticated, attractive people, and it is all too easy to want to emulate them.

The other path, though, is harder, one that requires intellectual and spiritual discipline. This path is one of prayer and meditation on God's teaching (*torah* in the Hebrew). The person who chooses this path delights in the *torah* of the LORD, and meditates on it day and night. The Hebrew verb translated here "meditates" (*hagah*) is the same word used in Isaiah 31:4 to describe a lion growling over its prey. Like a dog gnawing a particularly juicy bone, the person who meditates on God's word savors it, chewing it until it yields that which is life-giving. To borrow a phrase from Eugene Peterson, this is meditation as mastication.[2]

A well-known prayer from the Book of Common Prayer uses this same analogy between meditation and eating:

> Blessed Lord, who hast caused all holy Scriptures to be written for our learning; grant that we may in such wise hear them, read, mark, learn, and inwardly digest them, that by patience, and comfort of thy holy Word, we may embrace, and ever hold fast the blessed hope of everlasting life, which thou hast given us in our Savior Jesus Christ.[3]

"Read, mark, learn, and inwardly digest." This is a distinctly counter-cultural mode of learning in our world today. Who has the time or attention for such reading? According to a recent survey, the average American spends almost five hours a day on his or her smart phone and checks his or her social media accounts 17 times a day, at least once every waking hour.[4] We as a society get our news from sound bites and 280-character tweets. And we feed our egos by checking incessantly on how many "likes" our latest Facebook posts have garnered.

So what person in today's digitally connected, 24/7 world would do such a thing—reading slowly, reading and meditating on God's teaching day and night, chewing over it, inwardly digesting it? Well, hopefully, most of the people hearing or reading these words. We who are pastors and priests and teachers and lay leaders have the calling and the high privilege

---

2. I am adapting a phrase from Peterson's book, *Answering God: The Psalms as Tools for Prayer* (San Francisco: Harper & Row, 1989), 26.

3. *The Book of Common Prayer* (New York: Seabury, 1979), 184.

4. As reported in *Digital Trends*, a technology news website. The article can be read at http://www.digitaltrends.com/mobile/informate-report-social-media-smartphone-use/#:lFKnV5x-QcWG0A (accessed August 12, 2016).

of doing just that: studying God's word, meditating on it, praying with the psalmists and the prophets and the apostles, praying with Jesus.

My own dear teacher, Ellen Davis, in a sermon on Psalm 1, imagines the psalm as the instructions of a seminary teacher to her beloved students.[5] Do not walk in the way of the wicked or sit in the seat of scoffers. Delight in the *torah* of the Lord and meditate on it day and night.

The one who does that, says the psalmist, who studies Torah, studies the teaching of the Lord, will be "like a tree planted by streams of water, yielding its fruit in its season, and its leaves do not wither" (Ps 1:3).[6] Like a tree, planted by streams of water. What a lovely image: a tree whose roots are deep, nourished by flowing water; a tree which bears fruit in due season; a tree whose abundant foliage does not wither or wilt in the heat of the sun because it is connected by strong roots to the source of life, that is, well-watered soil.

The wicked, the mockers, on the other hand, says the psalmist, are like chaff, empty husks driven hither and yon by the wind. They have no roots, no substance, and finally, no lasting significance.

The choice is clear: be like a tree.

Now, a tree abundant in fruit and foliage is a lovely sight anywhere, but especially in a semiarid land like Israel. In that dry land, a green tree is a life-saver, quite literally. It is a sign that water is near. It is itself a source of shade, which can make the difference between life and death by sunstroke. It is also, of course, a source of nourishment for a weary traveler. A fresh, ripe fig, or a fragrant orange goes a long way toward restoring a tired person, body and soul.

So, the one who studies Torah, Holy Scripture, the one who allows Scripture to shape his or her prayers and life, is like such a tree, constantly connected to the source of life, abundant in fruit and foliage, providing shade and sustenance for a weary traveler.

Be like a tree.

Study, pray, be nourished by God's word, and (here's the point; here's where the tree imagery leads us) do it not just for yourself, but for those (students, parishioners) who will rest in your shade and be nourished by the fruit of your study.

5. Ellen F. Davis, *Wondrous Depth: Preaching the Old Testament* (Louisville: Westminster John Knox, 2005), 146–51. My own interpretation of the psalm is influenced by Davis's sermon.

6. Author's translation.

Be like a tree. Sink your roots deep into the well-watered soil that is Scripture, and you will bear fruit in due season.

Davis ends her sermon on Psalm 1 by quoting one of the many *be-rachot*, blessings said several times a day by observant Jews: "There is a short Jewish prayer that is said when someone catches sight of a particularly beautiful tree . . . *barûkh 'attah YHWH 'elohênû melekh ha'ôlam shekakhah lô be'ôlamô* . . . Blessed are you, O Lord, King of the Universe, who has something like this in his world."[7]

"Now imagine," Davis writes, "what if our own dedicated lives of prayer and meditation on God's Word would merit that same compliment for God—'Blessed are you, O Lord, King of the Universe, who has something like this in his world'? May it be so for each of us."[8]

It is a beautiful image of the praying life, the life of meditation on God's word. So, let's try it here. Let's be like a tree, rooted in God's word. Let's explore, in particular, some biblical texts about hope.

Hope

There are, as I said, many places one could look to in Scripture to think about hope: Jeremiah speaks God's promise to the exiles in Babylon: "Surely I know the plans I have for you, says the LORD, plans for your welfare and not for harm, to give you a future with hope" (Jer 29:11). Isaiah speaks to the same exiles,

> Do not fear, for I have redeemed you; I have called you by name, you are mine. When you pass through the waters, I will be with you; and through the rivers, they shall not overwhelm you; when you walk through fire you shall not be burned, and the flame shall not consume you. For I am the LORD your God, the Holy One of Israel, your Savior. (Isa 43:1–3)

The writer of Psalm 130 speaks of hope in the midst of grief, "I wait for the LORD, my soul waits, and in his word I hope; my soul waits for the Lord more than those who watch for the morning, more than those who watch for the morning. O Israel, hope in the LORD, for with the LORD there is steadfast love, and with him is great power to redeem" (Ps 130:5–7). And, of course, there is 1 Peter: "Always be ready to make your defense to

7. Davis, *Wondrous Depth*, 150.
8. Ibid., 150.

anyone who demands from you an accounting for the hope that is in you" (1 Pet 3:15).

Hope is a major theme in both the Old and New Testaments, but for the purposes of our time together I would like to talk about hope as it appears in the biblical narrative. I want to explore in particular two figures whose stories speak to me of hope: first Elijah, then Job.

Elijah at Mount Horeb

The biblical figure who came to mind for me first when I heard the theme for this volume, the "Emerging Christian Minority," was that crusty old prophet, Elijah, especially as he appears at Mount Horeb in 1 Kings 19.

You remember the story: Elijah has just had his most public victory yet over the prophets of Baal at Mount Carmel. But Elijah's triumph is short-lived. When Jezebel hears of the killing of her prophets, she sends a message to her nemesis: "So may the gods do to me, and more also, if I do not make your life like the life of one of them by this time tomorrow" (1 Kgs 19:2). Elijah runs for his life, from Israel in the north to Judah in the south, and then into the wilderness of the Negev, where he stops under a solitary tree, lies down, and wishes for death. "It is enough; now, O LORD, take away my life, for I am no better than my ancestors" (1 Kgs 19:4). He lies down and falls asleep. Then the angel of the LORD comes, wakes him up and says, of all things, "Get up and eat!" And lo and behold, there is something to eat in that barren wilderness—a cake baked on a hot stone and a jug of water where there had been nothing before. Get up. Eat. Drink. Here is bread for the journey.

Elijah obeys. He eats. He drinks. He sleeps again. And a second time, this very practical, almost motherly angel touches him and says, "Get up! Eat! Or the journey will be too much for you." Elijah eats again and drinks and then he retraces the journey of his recalcitrant ancestors across the wilderness of Sinai, traveling forty days and forty nights until he comes to the mountain of the LORD: Mount Sinai, Mount Horeb.

There, the word of the LORD comes to him and asks, "What are you doing here, Elijah?" And Elijah's answer is a well-documented extreme case of pastoral burnout: "I have been very zealous for the LORD, the God of hosts; for the Israelites have forsaken your covenant; they have thrown down your altars and put your prophets to the sword. I am left, I alone, and they are seeking my life to take it" (1 Kgs 19:9–10).[9]

Talk about feeling like a minority. I am left. I alone, and they are seeking my life. I am all you've got, LORD. I am all you've got, and I am not going to be around much longer.

The LORD, it seems, has had enough of Elijah's self-pity. So he tells Elijah to stand out on the mountain because the LORD is about to pass by. All the usual trappings of theophany—wind, earthquake, fire—pass by, but God is not in any of them. And then, the "still, small voice" "the sound of sheer silence"—the whisper of speech comes and Elijah knows, somehow he knows, that this is the moment, so he covers his face in his mantle and stands before the LORD, the God of hosts.

God says, again, "What are you doing here, Elijah?" But even the theophany he has just experienced does not move Elijah out of his depression. His answer is exactly the same as it was before: "I have been very zealous for the LORD, the God of hosts; for the Israelites have forsaken your covenant, thrown down your altars and put your prophets to the sword. I am left, I alone, and they are seeking my life to take it."

And then, God calls Elijah out of his self-pity, out of his depression, out of his extreme sense of isolation. God calls Elijah into vocation again, into life again: Go, Elijah, do what a prophet is supposed to do—anoint kings, anoint your successor. Go. Oh, and by the way, you are wrong, Elijah. There are 7,000 in Israel who have neither kneeled before Baal nor kissed him. You are not alone. I have appointed others to help you. Go, Elijah, do the work to which I have called you (1 Kgs 19:15–18).

Now, this story does not mention the word "hope." But I think it nevertheless teaches us some important things about hope. First, we are not alone. We are never alone. Truth be told, Elijah runs away not only from Jezebel, but also from his calling as a prophet. But he finds that he cannot escape God's presence. The psalmist's words might be his own: "Where can I go from your spirit? Or where can I flee from your presence? If I ascend to heaven, you are there. If I make my bed in Sheol, you are there. If I take the wings of the morning and settle at the farthest limits of the sea, even there your hand shall lead me, and your right hand shall hold me fast" (Ps 139:7–10).

Second, God gives us bread for the journey, that we might be strengthened for the tasks to which he calls us. Not a loaf baked on a hot stone and a

9. Author's translation.

jug of water, but the very bread of heaven and the cup of salvation: "This is my body, given for you. This is the blood of the new covenant, shed for you and for all people for the forgiveness of sins." Bread for the journey.

Third, God gives us the gift of vocation. And in the times when that vocation seems more like burden than gift, God calls us out of despair into life again. Sometimes that call is dramatic, a Damascus-road experience. Sometimes it is a sound of sheer silence. Sometimes it is the voice of a friend, a teacher, a parishioner, a student.

Lessons from Ethiopia

I think, for instance, of a student I taught three years ago. I was on sabbatical from Luther Seminary and my husband and I had decided that we wanted to meet our brothers and sisters in Christ across the world, so we spent the year in Addis Ababa, Ethiopia, where I taught at the Mekane Yesus Seminary and my husband, Doug, pastored a small English-speaking Lutheran church.

I taught in the M.A. program, and so all of the students I had were already pastors and evangelists. Many had several years of parish experience. One evening in class, the subject turned to the relationship between Christianity and culture. I told my students that I hesitated to use the term "missionary" for myself because that word had very negative connotations for many in American society. I explained that the history of missionaries is a mixed bag. Many were good people, but some were colonialists. Some did more harm than good. Some helped destroy indigenous cultures. But when I tried to acknowledge or confess those sins of the past, my students would hear none of it.

They told me instead about the great good that missionaries have done in Ethiopia over the last 150 years. They told me of a certain tribal group whose custom was to kill babies whose top teeth came in before their bottom teeth. "The missionaries saved those babies," they said. "They taught us not to be frightened of evil spirits." The students spoke of another tribal group whose culture dictates that a young man must kill a person before he is worthy of marriage. "The missionaries stopped that," they said, "and they worked to stop revenge killing." (Word to the wise: "culture" is not an unequivocal good. See "female circumcision.") When I spoke disparagingly about missionaries using Western styles of worship in Ethiopia, one student said, "But that's what they knew. You start with what you know."

Now, it must be noted that Ethiopia is the only African nation that was never colonized. Also, Ethiopia has been officially a Christian nation since the fourth century. The roots of the Ethiopian Orthodox Church run deep. The missionaries who arrived in the 19th century were not, by and large, colonialists. They evangelized largely among the non-Orthodox tribal groups of Ethiopia and were allowed to evangelize by the Ethiopian emperors primarily because they also built hospitals and schools. For all these reasons, the history of missions in Ethiopia differs from the history of missions in many other African nations. Still, the affection and respect shown to these missionaries by my students was striking.

We ended class that day with prayer, as was our custom. Then, as we were gathering up our things, Dagnaw, an evangelist of the Konso tribe from southern Ethiopia, stood up and spoke in his very deep, dignified voice:

"You tell those people," he said forcefully and with great emotion, "You tell those people that we highly value our missionaries. We honor those people who left their comfortable lives and brought Jesus to us. They left their comfortable lives back home and came to share our hard lives. They even lost some of their own children and buried them in our soil. We hold them in our hearts. You tell those people."

All I could say was, "I will, Dagnaw. I will." So I am.

Or I think of another student, Galgalo Elema, whom I taught while he was a student at Luther Seminary. Galgalo invited us to visit him in Awassa, a town southwest of Addis Ababa, where he serves as the dean of a regional seminary that is bursting at the seams with students. As we ate in his home, he reflected on his time in the United States studying at Luther Seminary. Galgalo highly valued his education at Luther, but he was troubled by a visit he had made to a church in Minneapolis early in his time there. This church was concerned with social ministry and did wonderful work with Muslim refugees, but the members and the pastor did not, by and large, speak about Jesus to the refugees for fear of being coercive. Galgalo found this a troubling and strange set of affairs.

"The church," he said to us, "is the only group of people called to proclaim the gospel. That is what we do. A lot of organizations provide humanitarian aid. We do, too. We minister to the whole person. But we are the only people whose task it is to proclaim the gospel of Jesus Christ. If we do not proclaim the gospel, then we are just like any other organization. If we do not proclaim the gospel, we are not the church."

My own American students could learn much from Galgalo and Dagnaw and other African Christians. Lately, in reading my American students' papers, I've noticed that they are fond of a saying attributed erroneously to St. Francis: "Preach the gospel at all times. If necessary, use words." Putting aside the fact that St. Francis himself was a prolific preacher, this is not the problem of the mainline Protestant churches today, including mine. There are undoubtedly churches who need to live out in action what they preach. The problem with the mainline churches is the opposite: they often do not preach what they live out. We in the mainline need to actually preach the gospel with actions *and* with words. We need to name the name of Jesus. We need to name the hope that we have in Jesus Christ.

Here is the point: God calls us to proclaim the gospel. God calls us to vocation and when we lose hope, when we feel that we are the only faithful ones left, God calls us back, again and again. And God gives us companions for the journey. We have much to learn, for instance, from the church in Africa. The Mekane Yesus church in Ethiopia is the fastest-growing Lutheran church body in the world. In the last fifty-plus years, the church has grown from 20,000 members to 7 million members. They grew by 1 million members just in the last three years. And all of their primary leaders are Ethiopian. Missionaries continue to work alongside the Mekane Yesus Church, but their passion for sharing the gospel is their own, and they do it much more effectively than any Western church I know, despite a lack of material resources. And they are not alone. The church is growing by leaps and bounds all over Africa. According to the Pew Research Center, nearly two-thirds of the world's Christians now live in the Global South.[10] The center of gravity of Christianity has shifted to Africa and South America and Asia.

So when we feel despair or discouragement, when we become Elijah on Mount Horeb—I am left, I alone—we should remember this: we are not alone. God's Spirit is alive and well and moving in our world today. And God continues to call us back into vocation, to proclaim God's redeeming love for the whole world in Jesus Christ, through the power of the Holy Spirit.

10. From "Global Christianity—A Report on the Size and Distribution of the World's Christian Population" by the Pew Research Center (2011). Find a summary of the report at http://www.pewforum.org/2011/12/19/global-christianity-exec/ (accessed August 13, 2016).

The Book of Job

Another book, another example of hope. This time it is that man of sorrows, God's servant Job.

It may seem counterintuitive to study Job to talk about hope. In the long dialogue with his companions that occupies the core of the book, Job emphatically says several times that he has no hope: "My days are swifter than a weaver's shuttle and come to their end without hope" (Job 7:6). "The mountain falls and crumbles away, and the rock is removed from its place; the waters wear away the stones; the torrents wash away the soil of the earth; so you destroy the hope of mortals" (Job 14:18–19).

Job's friends are uncomfortable, to say the least, with such sentiments. They speak several times about hope, trying to inspire it in Job. "Your life will be brighter than the noonday; its darkness will be like the morning," predicts Zophar, "And you will have confidence, because there is hope" (Job 11:17–18). Eliphaz also challenges Job, "Is not your fear of God your confidence, and the integrity of your ways your hope" (Job 4:6)? And it is true that Job holds to his integrity, but as it turns out, in the end that is not the source of his hope.

Before we can talk about the source of Job's hope, though, we must acknowledge the depths of his despair. Job, even more than Elijah, feels alone in the world, and with good reason. Job's world has descended into chaos through no fault of his own. He has lost his wealth, his health, and all his children in one fell swoop. And his so-called friends just add insult to injury, calling on him to repent of whatever evil he must have done to deserve this punishment.

But worst of all, God has turned against Job, and this is the betrayal that he cannot bear. God the creator, the one who knit Job together in his mother's womb, is at one and the same time God the destroyer, the lion, the warrior, who stalks Job with deadly intent. Job's language is paradoxical and almost breaks apart under the strain of trying to grasp who this God is. He speaks in stark terms: "He will slay me. I have no hope. But I will defend my ways to his face" (Job 13:15).

So Job plummets into the pit of despair, lamenting to his friends, and, as time passes, lamenting more and more to God:

> Am I the Sea or the Dragon, that you set a guard over me? When
> I say, "My bed will comfort me, my couch will ease my complaint,"
> then you scare me with dreams and terrify me with visions, so

> that I would choose strangling and death rather than this body
> . . .What are human beings, that you make so much of them, that
> you set your mind on them, visit them every morning, test them
> every moment? Will you not look away from me for a while, let me
> alone until I swallow my spit? (Job 7:12–15, 17–19)

In the midst of this despair, though, there are moments when Job speaks of a strange hope that bursts out of him almost against his will. In chapter 14, for instance, Job speaks of death, and the finality of death:

> For there is hope for a tree, if it is cut down, that it will sprout
> again, and that its shoots will not cease . . . But mortals die, and are
> laid low; humans expire, and where are they? As waters fail from
> a lake, and a river wastes away and dries up, so mortals lie down
> and do not rise again; until the heavens are no more, they will not
> awake or be roused out of their sleep. (Job 14:7, 10–12)

There is hope for a tree, but not for human beings, according to Job.

In the next breath, though, Job holds out something like hope that God will yet have mercy on him:

> Oh that you would hide me in Sheol, that you would conceal me
> until your wrath is past, that you would appoint me a set time, and
> remember me! If mortals die, will they live again? All the days of
> my service I would wait until my release should come. You would
> call, and I would answer you; you would long for the work of your
> hands. (Job 14:13–15)

"Oh that you would hide me in Sheol," Job cries, and it is a striking image. Sheol, the underworld, the place of death, becomes a safe place, a hiding place, a place where Job can wait until God's anger is past, until God longs for him again.

This strange hope in the pit of despair that characterizes some of Job's speech breaks out most famously in chapter 19:

> O that my words were written down! O that they were inscribed in
> a book! O that with an iron pen and with lead they were engraved
> on a rock forever! For I know that my Redeemer lives, and that at
> the last he will stand upon the earth; and after my skin has been
> thus destroyed, then in my flesh I shall see God, whom I shall
> see on my side, and my eyes shall behold, and not another. (Job
> 19:23–27)

The identity of the "redeemer" in Job's most famous speech is unclear. What is clear is that Job espouses some hope of vindication. Whether in this life or after he dies, he hopes for his redeemer to vindicate him. In the pit of despair, he is not alone. There is one who will speak for him.

Perhaps Job's greatest hope is this: "And after my skin has been thus destroyed, then in my flesh *I shall see God.*" And that, finally, is where Job's hope lies. Eliphaz had asked him: "Is not the integrity of your ways your hope?" And it is. He does hold to his integrity, fiercely. He has not sinned, and he knows that. He will not lie, to himself, to his friends, or to God. But here, finally, is where his hope lies: that the God he knows, the God who fashioned him in his mother's womb and has been his God throughout his life, that this God will show up and will answer him. Job ends his speech this way: "O that I had one to hear me! Here is my signature! Let the Almighty answer me" (Job 31:35)! And, of course, at the end of the book, the Almighty does show up. Against all odds, the Almighty shows up and answers Job.

The great God-speeches at the end of the book of Job have garnered many different interpretations. Some people read them as God brow-beating Job over the head with creation. William Safire says, "It is as if God appears in a tie-dyed T-shirt emblazoned with the words 'Because I'm God, That's Why.'"[11] I do not read the speeches that way. I read them as God putting Job in his place, certainly. "Where were you when I laid the foundation of the earth?" God says, and Job learns that he is not the center of the universe. The world does not revolve around him. Job, in other words, learns humility from these speeches. He is taken out to where the wild things are and he understands for the first time that it is not all about him. In this new world, he learns what it means to be a part of God's creation along with all the other wonderful, wild creatures that inhabit it.

But there is something else here besides a lesson in humility. I read the divine speeches more as invitation than as confrontation. Where were you? God says. Are you able? Do you know? God puts Job in his place, but Job is also the only passenger on this whirlwind tour of the cosmos, and God shows off the depths of the sea and the glory of the Pleiades and the impenetrable scales of Leviathan with apparent delight and pride.

Job learns humility, but Job also learns wonder, to delight in creation as God does. Job is called out of his all-too-understandable preoccupation

11. William Safire, *The First Dissident: The Book of Job in Today's Politics* (New York: Random House, 1992), 22.

with his loss and his grief into a world that is bigger and wilder and more beautiful than he ever imagined.

Perhaps we as the church need to learn both humility and wonder, too. Perhaps we need to be decentered. As in the Copernican revolution, we need to realize that we are not the center of the universe, that we are not anymore the center of society. We need to learn the hard lesson of humility. But we are also invited to wonder.

Job is called out of his preoccupation with loss and grief into a world that is bigger and wilder and more beautiful than he ever imagined. We, as the church, are also called out (the root meaning of *ecclesia*), called out from our grief and our mourning for what was, called out from the remnants of Christendom to a world that is risky and wild, but also beautiful and full of possibilities for faithful action and irrepressible hope.

At the end of the book, Job responds to this vision of the divine speeches by acknowledging what he did not understand before: "I had heard of you by the hearing of the ear," he says, "but now my eye sees you" (Job 42:5). Somehow, in the vision of the vast beautiful world that God has created, Job has seen God, and thus his hope is fulfilled. Remember that back in chapter 19, Job had hoped for just such a vision: "I know that my Redeemer lives. And that at the last he will stand upon the earth; and after my skin has been thus destroyed, then in my flesh I shall see God" (Job 19:26).

At the end of the book, this vision of God enables Job to finally move out of his grief and his despair into life again. God restores his fortunes and gives him ten children again. This last action seems a cheap trick to many: How can you replace children?

Ellen Davis reads the ending of the book of Job differently: "It is useless to ask how much (or how little) it costs God to give more children. The real question is how much it costs Job to become a father again."[12] What does it cost Job to risk that kind of heartbreak again, knowing the pain that is implicit in loving children in all their beauty and in all their vulnerability? The most courageous thing Holocaust survivors ever did, Davis argues, is to have children after the cataclysm, bringing children into a world capable of such evil, risking love again, risking life again.[13]

12. Ellen F. Davis, *Getting Involved with God Rediscovering the Old Testament* (Cambridge, MA: Cowley, 2001), 142. Davis's chapter on Job, "The Sufferer's Wisdom," is the best theological essay on Job that I know of. My interpretation of Job 42, the epilogue, is heavily influenced by Davis's reading.

13. Ibid., 141.

But that is exactly what Job and his wife do. They risk loving again. They risk living again. And Job names his three beautiful daughters Dove, Cinnamon Stick, and Rouge Pot and he gives them an inheritance along with their brothers, an act unheard of in the ancient Near East. Job learns to parent as God does—giving his children the freedom to become who they are created to be. And in this way he begins to live again.

Go back to Job 19. "I know that my Redeemer lives," Job proclaims out of the depths of despair, "And that at the last he will stand upon the earth and after my skin has been thus destroyed, then in my flesh I shall see God." Job may or may not be talking about resurrection when he says that. But what Job most certainly voices is hope, flashes of inexplicable hope in the midst of despair, hope founded on his past experience of God's faithfulness, and hope founded, finally, on the vision of the God of life who finally reveals himself to Job at the end of the book. For that reason, he can risk living again and loving again, even in spite of the unexplained and inexplicable suffering he has endured.

And that, in the end, even in the midst of anxiety and despair, is where our hope lies as well—in Job's God, in our God, who is the God of life.

Resurrection Hope

Let me illustrate with another anecdote: I was teaching a class on Jewish-Christian relations a few years ago with a Jewish friend of mine, Jonathan Paradise, a retired professor from the University of Minnesota. One of the students in the class had recently visited Israel and had a question for him.

"I was on the bus," the student explained, "and I overheard two men talking. The one said, 'Abraham, may he rest in peace . . .' Is that a common way to talk about biblical characters?"

"Oh, yes," Jonathan replied, "In Israel, you'll often hear people talk about Abraham and Sarah as if they were talking about their own parents: 'Uncle Morris, may he rest in peace. Abraham, may he rest in peace.' It is interesting; I don't hear Christians say things like that. I've never heard a Christian say, 'Paul, may he rest in peace. Peter, may he rest in peace. Jesus, may he rest in peace.'"

We all let that sink in for a moment and then everyone burst out laughing, including Jonathan. And I said, "No, we definitely would never say, 'Jesus, may he rest in peace.' That would pretty much nullify everything that we believe in."

It was an unintended joke that illustrates a crucial point: our hope as Christians finally rests on this—the cross and the resurrection of Jesus Christ. "If for this life only we have hoped in Christ," says Paul, "we are of all people most to be pitied" (1 Cor 15:19). That is a stark and sobering statement. But then Paul goes on to proclaim resurrection faith in a rising crescendo of hope: "But in fact Christ has been raised from the dead, the first fruits of those who have died. For since death came through a human being, the resurrection of the dead has also come through a human being. For as all die in Adam, so all will be made alive in Christ" (1 Cor 15:20–22).

Now, it may seem strange for a Lutheran to be focusing on the resurrection. After all, Lutherans are all about the theology of the cross, right? "A theologian of the cross," says Luther, "calls the thing what it actually is."[14] Let's call the thing, then, what it actually is: we are not in Christendom anymore. We are not the center of society anymore. And that is probably a good thing. We follow a crucified God and our power is not political power or economic power; our power is the power of the cross, the power of suffering love. The current situation of the church in North America serves to remind us of this fundamental theological truth.

The cross is essential to our identity as Christians. Christian theology cannot, however, end at the cross. If the cross is the end of the matter, then the suffering and death of Jesus becomes just another case of the good dying young, and we are left with no particular hope other than a God who feels our pain. While misery loves company, such comfort is a cold comfort.

Belief in the resurrection, the resurrection of Jesus and our own resurrections, is what ultimately redeems our suffering. This kind of theology has been denigrated as a "pie in the sky by and by" kind of hope. And it *is* problematic if that belief in the next life leads one to be passive in the face of great evil in this life. If Job teaches us anything, it is that one cannot be quiet or passive in the face of great suffering, and certainly not in the face of great evil. Job is anything but a quietist.

In other words, if one's hope in resurrection is simply for the next life, then one is left to get through this life in the best way possible and wait like an audience member for the curtain to come up on the real drama. But that's not what belief in the resurrection does, or should do. Belief in the resurrection claims that God is a God of life, and that even in the face

14. *Luther's Works*, American Edition, 55 vols., eds., J. Pelikan and H. Lehmann (St. Louis and Philadelphia: Concordia and Fortress, 1955), 31:45.

of great suffering and death, God works life in us and through us, for *this* world, right here, right now, *and* for the world to come.

Christians do not seek out suffering. We are not masochists. But we encounter the suffering that comes our way with the knowledge that nothing can separate us from the love of God in Christ Jesus, not even suffering or death itself. And so we are freed to enter into our own and others' suffering, knowing that God has gone there before us and is there with us, and that God will bring life even out of the darkest situation.

Job says, "I know that my Redeemer lives. And at the last he shall stand upon the earth; and after my skin has been thus destroyed, then in my flesh I shall see God." This passage probably does not espouse a full-fledged belief in resurrection, at least not originally, but Job's story of new life after unspeakable tragedy participates in the broader Old Testament narrative of reversal—the poor lifted up, slaves set free, exiles brought home—the narrative that eventually finds fullest expression in the doctrine of the resurrection of the dead. Jon Levenson writes this of the restoration of Job; though it is not resurrection of the dead,

> It is a reversal nonetheless, the replacement of despair with hope, of gloom with shining light. It was such a reversal in the same direction, a restoration in the same direction, that the rabbis (along with their Pharisaic antecedents and Christian contemporaries) expected in the future resurrection of the dead.[15]

Given this theme of reversal in the book of Job, we should not be surprised to see the hope of resurrection made explicit in the LXX translation of Job. The LXX translators added this detail to the end of the book: "And Job died, old and full of days. *And it is written that he will rise again with those whom the Lord raises up.*"

Death and Resurrection

Resurrection faith, of course, neither negates nor denies the reality of death. The doctrine of the resurrection, as orthodox Jewish and Christian theology understands it, is not the same as the idea of the immortality of the soul. Resurrection is not a natural process, as inevitable as the renewal of the earth in springtime. Death is real and final. Resurrection is only possible

---

15. Jon Levenson, *Resurrection and the Restoration of Israel: The Ultimate Victory of the God of Life* (New Haven: Yale University Press, 2006), 70.

through the direct intervention of the God of life. It is a hard-fought battle, not an easy road, as we learn only too well from Job's story.

It is this last insight that inspired, I think, William Blake's penultimate depiction of Job in his 1826 series of engravings on the book. In this engraving, Job is surrounded by his three beautiful daughters and behind him on the wall are scenes from earlier in the book. On his right and left are scenes of destruction, the loss of his flocks and herds and servants described in chapter 1. Directly behind him is the scene of God speaking out of the whirlwind, Job and his wife and three companions bowing low in awe.

There are a few things to note about this particular engraving. First, Job bears a striking resemblance to God—they have the same face, the same hair and beard, and they hold their arms in the same posture. Second, that posture is in a cruciform shape—both God and Job hold their arms out in blessing, perhaps, but also in the shape of a cross. At the very bottom of the engraving, Blake quotes Psalm 139:8, "If I ascend into Heaven thou art there. If I make my bed in Hell behold Thou art there."

Blake, it seems to me, has captured in this engraving the tension between the all-too-present reality of suffering and death and the promise of resurrection. The last engraving in his series is fully about resurrection and new life—Job and his restored family play music and dance as the sun rises. But in this penultimate sketch, Job blesses his beautiful daughters in imitation of God while he also remembers the road that has brought him to this moment, from death and unspeakable suffering to new life.

Just as Jesus, even after his resurrection, still bears the wounds of his death on the cross (Luke 24:39–40, John 20:19–29), so Blake's Job bears the wounds of his suffering. In both instances, however, as so many believers through the years have proclaimed, suffering and death do not have the final word. "If I ascend into Heaven, you are there. If I make my bed in Sheol you are there," says the ancient Israelite psalmist. "I know that my Redeemer lives," cries Job out of the pit of death. "But, in fact, Christ has been raised from the dead," Paul preaches. All of these biblical writers proclaim faith in the God of Israel, the God of life, who is faithful even until death, and beyond.

So, in the midst of death and indifference and outright hostility, in the midst of the disconcerting changes in society and the loss of Christendom, we do not worry, we do not engage in self-pity, we do not lose heart. Instead, we have hope. God is faithful. Paul writes to the church in Rome:

> Therefore, since we are justified by faith, we have peace with God through our Lord Jesus Christ, through whom we have obtained access to this grace in which we stand; and we boast in our hope of sharing the glory of God. And not only that, but we also boast in our sufferings, knowing that suffering produces endurance, and endurance produces character, and character produces hope, and hope does not disappoint us, because God's love has been poured into our hearts through the Holy Spirit that has been given to us. (Rom 5:1–5)

With roots firmly planted in the soil of God's word, we have hope. Not because of anything that we can do, but because of what God has already done. The God who called Elijah out of despair into vocation, the God who called Job from death into life, the God who became flesh in Jesus the Christ, the God who suffered death and was buried and on the third day rose again, this is the same God who calls us out of despair into hope.

Paul ends that wonderful chapter on resurrection, 1 Corinthians 15, with this resounding proclamation:

> This perishable body must put on imperishability, and this mortal body must put on immortality. When this perishable body puts on imperishability, and this mortal body puts on immortality, then the saying that is written will be fulfilled: "Death has been swallowed up in victory. Where, O death, is your victory? Where, O death, is your sting?" The sting of death is sin, and the power of sin is the law. But thanks be to God, who gives us the victory through our Lord Jesus Christ. (1 Cor 15:53–57)

This is the foundation of our hope, and it has implications for how we live out our vocations. Because Paul doesn't stop here; he moves to a "therefore." *Because* Jesus has been raised from the dead, *because* we too shall be resurrected, *because* death has lost its sting, "*Therefore*, my beloved, be steadfast, immovable, always excelling in the work of the Lord, because you know that in the Lord *your labor is not in vain*" (1 Cor 15:58).

And *that* is a word of hope. Thanks be to God.

5

Professing the Faith in "A Secular Age"[1]

Joseph D. Small

But how are they to call on one in whom they have not believed?
And how are they to believe in one of whom they have never
heard? And how are they to hear without someone to proclaim
him? And how are they to proclaim him unless they are sent?

ROMANS 10:14–15

"The first Christians he met as a boy in Korea were Adventist missionaries, very simple people. They had no power and wanted no
power. They told us Bible stories, it is true. But they gave us food
and shelter and medicine first, and told us jokes and played with
us and loved us. So we *begged* them for the stories." He laughed
again. "This is what Joon thought Christianity meant! Food and
medicine for the body, and stories for the heart if you begged for
them. Then he came here, found a country full of people begging
not to hear the stories, went to seminary, and found out why. No
food. No medicine. No doing unto others. Just a bunch of men
learning how to bellow the stories at others whether they wanted
to hear them or not!"

DAVID JAMES DUNCAN, THE BROTHERS K[2]

---

1. This essay originally appeared in Joseph Small, *Flawed Church, Faithful God* (Grand
Rapids: Eerdmans, 2017). Reprinted by permission of the publisher; all rights reserved.

2. James David Duncan, *The Brothers K* (New York: Bantam, 1992), 60f.

Public Square and Private Faith

In the early 1980s, Richard John Neuhaus published an influential book with a provocative title: *The Naked Public Square*. At the time, Neuhaus was a Lutheran pastor who occupied some space in the public square, but it was *The Naked Public Square* that made him a widely recognized public figure. Neuhaus lamented the retreat of religion into private life and the exclusion of religion and religiously grounded values from the conduct of public business. He asserted that prevailing "political doctrine and practice" had resulted in public space emptied of the positive presence of religious values and religious social critique. He attributed the religious absence from public life to a dominant political doctrine—America as a secular society—that asserted freedom from sectarian religious interference. This doctrine, he maintained, found dogmatic expression in "the ideology of secularism," that assumed a high wall of separation between church and state.[3]

Reading *The Naked Public Square* more than three decades after its publication provides an interesting perspective on the current state of American "political doctrine and practice" and on the population of the public square. In the 1980s, Neuhaus believed that, "We are witnessing today a contention between religious groups—evangelical, fundamentalist, Catholic—to succeed mainline Protestantism as the culture-shaping force that provides moral legitimacy for democracy in America."[4] He was right that mainline Protestantism no longer provides moral legitimacy for democracy, but what he did not envision is the rapid expansion of religious (and non-religious) pluralism in America. Not only has increased religious and moral diversity expanded far beyond Christian options, but pluralism has also accelerated religion's retreat into the private sphere, consigning it to an even smaller space in a remote corner of the public square.

More than two decades ago, historian Mark Noll also published an influential book with a provocative title: *The Scandal of the Evangelical Mind*. The book's first sentence was even more provocative: "The scandal of the evangelical mind is that there is not much of an evangelical mind."[5] Noll's critique came from within evangelicalism, but it was consistent with broader assessments about the shallowness of Christian thought in Amer-

3. Richard John Neuhaus, *The Naked Public Square: Religion and Democracy in America* (Grand Rapids: Eerdmans, 1984), vii.

4. Ibid., vii.

5. Mark Noll, *The Scandal of the Evangelical Mind* (Grand Rapids: Eerdmans, 1994), 3.

ica's churches. Douglas John Hall, taking note of the statistical symptoms of Christendom's waning, asserted that grim numbers provide only superficial accounts of the situation. He believed that something more serious is at stake in the church. "No doubt, certain statistical and other aspects of that deeper malaise are made visible through the activities of pollsters and popular sociologists," Hall wrote, "but the crisis behind the crisis cannot be submitted to computer programming. For that rudimentary crisis is *a crisis of thinking*."[6]

Noll and Hall represent a consistent, decades-long identification of diminishing ecclesial attention to the theological and ethical core of Christian faith and life. Their criticism of churchly inattention to the profound truths of the gospel, resulting in such thin beliefs as "Moral Therapeutic Deism" and "prosperity gospels" may be nothing new. Perhaps every generation echoes Luther's cry that church members and their pastors "know absolutely nothing about the Christian faith," but traditional lament about thin faith within the church is now coupled with diminished cultural interest in the faith and moral values of the churches.

A Secular Age

None of this comes as news to us. We see contracted public presence and thinned out faith as symptomatic of secularity: the marginalization of Christian churches as they, along with other religious institutions, are pushed to the periphery of the public square, coupled with an evident decline in Christian belief and practice. It is true enough that Christmas has given way to "the Holidays," that Easter is now marked by "Spring break," and that the churches are no longer influential actors in political and societal arenas. It is also true enough that the religious faith of American Christian teenagers, and the churches that shape their faith, is marked by a generic deity's therapeutic support for conventional morality. But these signs of secularity—public spaces emptied of significant religious presence, and the thinning out of fully Christian belief and practice—are themselves only symptoms of a deeper problem for the church.

Charles Taylor's monumental study, *A Secular Age*, focuses on the cultural conditions that affect religious belief. He characterizes the shift to secularity in the West as "a move from a society where belief in God is

6. Douglas John Hall, *Thinking the Faith: Christian Theology in a North American Context* (Minneapolis, MN: Augsburg, 1989), 12.

unchallenged and, indeed, unproblematic, to one in which it is understood to be one option among others, and frequently not the easiest to embrace."[7] Taylor tells the story of this shift in a tour de force that ranges over 500 years and takes nearly 800 pages to narrate. While some of the details in Taylor's story may be arguable, his depiction of the pervasive *experience* of our secular age is all too recognizable.

What does it mean to say that we live in a secular age? Taylor is not interested in demonizing "secularism," but rather in describing "our contemporary lived understanding; that is, the way we naïvely take things to be." Not "naïve" in the sense of simple, credulous, and artless belief, but more precisely as, "the construal we just live in, without ever being aware of it as a construal, or—for most of us—without ever formulating it."[8] Taylor wants to uncover our straightforward, embedded experience of *the way things are.* This naïve experience can be discerned in our everyday engagement in commercial, political, cultural, educational, professional, and recreational activities. The way we function in each of these areas of life, the norms we follow and the deliberations we engage in, are commonly shaped by prevailing societal assumptions and practices. The routine, everyday choices we make do not typically refer to God or to religious beliefs, but to the taken-for-granted, widely shared understanding of life in twenty-first-century America. The "we" Taylor speaks of in all of this does not include every single person, of course, but "we" encompasses religious as well as nonreligious persons. The "we" also encompasses much of the life of American churches. Churches make decisions and engage in economic, planning, marketing, and political activities that are shaped by prevailing social rationalities, with only habitual, de rigueur reference to the gospel.

Taylor gives needed nuance to the standard narrative of secularity. He notes that "Everyone can see that there have been declines in practice and declared belief in many countries, particularly in recent decades, that God is not present in public space as in past centuries, and so on for a host of other changes . . . But how to understand and interpret these changes may not be evident."[9] Taylor moves beyond what everyone can see to explore the resulting vulnerabilities of religion and religious faith. What does it mean

---

7. Charles Taylor, *A Secular Age* (Cambridge, MA: Belknap Press/Harvard University Press, 2007), 3.

8. Ibid., 30.

9. Ibid., 426.

that in our time and place, belief in God is understood to be one option among others, and frequently not the easiest to embrace?

A central experience of our secular age is the lived understanding that moral aspirations and worthy lives do not necessarily originate from God or intend toward God. Rather, we all live in a time when it is widely understood that moral goals can be related to many different motivations, only some of which may be religious. Furthermore, commendable moral aims are most often dedicated solely to human flourishing, requiring no god to inspire them and no god to give them purpose. One statistical indication of this reality is the steady decline in the percentage of charitable giving to religious causes. Altruistic generosity no longer flows naturally from religious motivation through religious channels. The Bill and Melinda Gates Foundation is typical, declaring its aim to "help all people live healthy, productive lives." Whatever Bill and Melinda Gates's religious convictions may or may not be, they have no discernable impact on the origin, goals, and initiatives of their forty-billion-dollar foundation. It is not only lofty purpose that is at issue, however. What is true of noble moral aspirations is also true of more commonplace, day-to-day ambitions and plans. In neither high purposes nor quotidian aims is obligation or gratitude to God a natural or necessary component in the choices we make daily.

In our secular age, believers in a transcendent God experience a social setting in which many others live quite contentedly with negligible or no religious faith. Most of them are ordinary people who live conventional lives, some are virtuous people who live honorable lives, others are self-serving people whose lives are more or less disreputable, but all of them manage their lives without reference to the transcendent. "A secular age," says Taylor, "is one in which the eclipse of all goals beyond human flourishing . . . falls within the range of an imaginable life for masses of people."[10] Whether it is the flourishing of the self alone or the flourishing of a community, a nation, or the planet, the unquestioned focus is on the immanent, the here and now, and what we humans can bring about.

While it is obvious enough that in our secular age there is an increase in aggressive atheism and explicit agnosticism, more typical is the growing number of people who experience no need for religious faith. A recent novel narrates the unexpected, unconventional conversion to Christian faith of a young woman, Sophie Wilder. Sophie's new-found Catholicism is

10. Ibid., 19f.

a puzzle to her friends, even to Sophie herself. One of the people in her life responds to Sophie's new faith with sarcasm:

> "It's funny," he said. "After all this time, people still can't do without God. I never would have guessed that He'd survive to your genera-tion. Even the atheists are militant. They can't quite get over Him."

> "Most of my friends don't think one way or another about it," So-phie told him. "They're not for or against it; they're just beyond it."[11]

In our secular age, religious belief in general, and Christian belief in particular, is only an option within a variety of possibilities for arranging one's life, one that many have just moved beyond. Nonreligious possibilities reflect what Taylor calls "exclusive humanism": living a meaningful human life within a closed, self-sufficient universe. Taylor's "exclusive humanism" is not the demonic "secular humanism" of popular Christian mythology, but simply ordinary life that may be decent, even virtuous, without reference to God or to any transcendent reality, and certainly without the church. Ex-clusive humanism is not one thing, but many things "which leave no place for the 'vertical' or 'transcendent,' but which in one way or another close these off, render them inaccessible, or even unthinkable."[12] So, this "secular age" is characterized by the lived experience of a horizontal, immanent, self-sufficient world that has no apparent need for anything beyond the hu-man to provide a satisfying life.

It is crucial to recognize that a secular age is not one in which reli-gious people experience their lives as fully derived from God and directed to God, in contrast to secular people who arrange their lives without refer-ence to the transcendent. Religious people, and the subset of committed Christian people, are immersed in a secular age characterized by the as-sumption of human self-sufficiency. In this secularized society, belief itself becomes more challenging. Stripped of what Peter Berger calls "plausibility structures"[13]—the social and cultural supports for transcendent faith—churches can no longer assume that people will be drawn into or kept within a faith by a strong ecclesial or cultural identity, or by the sense that they are participating in a transcendent social ethic. "The tight normative

11. Christopher R. Beha, *What Happened to Sophie Wilder* (Portland, OR: Tin House, 2012), 85.

12. Taylor, *Secular Age*, 556.

13. Peter Berger, *The Sacred Canopy*, (Garden City, NY: Doubleday, 1967).

link between a certain religious identity, the belief in certain theological propositions, and a standard practice, no longer holds for a great number of people," says Taylor. "Many of these are engaged in assembling their own personal outlook, through a kind of bricolage."[14] All of this holds for a great number of Christian people as well. And so, while "believing without belonging" may characterize some outside of the church, it may be that *within* the church, "belonging without believing" is a consequence of our secular age. The primary mission field is not North America as the missional folk say, but the churches themselves.

Proclaiming the Gospel in a Secular Age

All of this has obvious implications for proclaiming the gospel and shaping life within Christian communities of faith. Churches are no longer culturally sanctioned and can no longer rely on attractional strategies to draw people through their doors. Positioning themselves as alluring religious options is less and less likely to appeal to people who see no need for the multiple programs and opportunities the churches offer. As challenging as this reality is for the church, other implications of life in a secular age are even more fundamental. For example, to a great extent the churches themselves—their officials, priests, and members—have come to share the assumptions and practices of the secular setting in which we all live and move and have our being.

Nonreligious descriptions of reality are the underlying assumptions shared throughout modern, Western societies. These taken-for-granted secular notions of "the way things are" find themselves at home in the churches, although they are partially concealed under a patina of religious rhetoric. Denominational divisions in America, as well as "progressive-evangelical" divides, are tempered by common allegiance to the values, motivations, and aims that characterize a secular age. There is a sense in which this is understandable. Christians and their churches are not only *in* the world, but also, in substantial measure, *of* the world. We pray to God, "thy kingdom come," but we live in a world, and a church, characterized by reliance on human wisdom and action to bring about desired social and ecclesial ends.

And so our marginalized churches are not only disestablished culturally, but find the very shape of their Christian faith and life affected by the

14. Ibid., 514.

secular age in which they live. This is "natural" in the sense that church people breathe the same cultural air that everyone else breathes, but it is also
"intentional" in the sense that churches appeal to our secular age's increas-
ingly disinterested populace by seeking to demonstrate their correspondence to secular rationality. Theology, worship, morality, programming,
evangelism, mission, and church governance assume an understanding
of reality that *all* people share—religious and nonreligious alike—and to
which the church can and should appeal. But this comes with a cost.

David Hollinger's incisive studies of Protestantism include the telling observation that children of mainline Protestant churches "found that
Christianity was not so indispensable to the advancement of the values
most energetically taught to them" by their churches.[15] To the extent that
the churches speak and act merely as a religious version of aims pursued
by numerous nonreligious organizations and institutions (usually more effectively), loyalty to the church becomes optional, even extraneous. Liberal
Protestantism, says Hollinger, "enabled its community of faith to serve,
among its other roles, as a commodious halfway house to what for lack of a
better term we can call post-Protestant secularism."[16]

How, then, is the church to proclaim the gospel in "A Secular Age?"
The answer begins with a negation. The church must first turn away from
its characteristic proclamation of itself—marketing its attractive suite of religious goods and services—and turn toward God's new Way in the world,
the Way in and through Jesus Christ, crucified, risen, and ascended. But
how is this to be done in our secular age, when fewer and fewer people are
interested in what the church has to say? Even a strengthened, clarified, unified proclamation of the gospel is easily lost in the cacophony of conflict-
ing messages proclaiming alternate "salvations," from hedonism through
self-improvement to narcissistic mysticism, from expanding rights through
genetic engineering to saving the planet. Even at its best, the church is but
one voice in a world inundated with words. In an age when religious faith
in general and Christian faith in particular is but one option among many,
and not the easiest to embrace, how is the gospel to be heard, and how will
hearing lead to faith?

15. David A. Hollinger, *After Cloven Tongues of Fire: Protestant Liberalism in Modern American History* (Princeton, NJ: Princeton University Press, 2013), 44.
16. Ibid., 46.

The Church's Proclamation of the Gospel in a Previous Age

It is often said that the religious and secular pluralism of twenty-first-century America resembles the Greco-Roman religious and philosophical pluralism in which the early church grew. It is then proposed that the solution to the church's current proclamation dilemma is to emulate the early church so that the contemporary church will be strengthened in faith and increase in numbers daily (cf. Acts 6:7; 9:31; 12:24; 16:5; 19:20; 28:30–31). Recourse to the Book of Acts encourages bold proclamation, persuasive apologetics, and heroic missionary endeavors. Peter and Paul are the models; it is thought that their *kerygma*, their *didachē*, their travels and church planting provide the prototype for twenty-first-century church growth. However, using Acts as the model does not provide a complete or even typical picture of the church's three centuries of growth from a tiny Jewish sect to the favored religion of the empire. Something more than heroic apostolic action was at work.

Alan Kreider gives voice to a scholarly consensus that, "According to the evidence at our disposal, the expansion of the church was not organized, the product of a mission program; it simply happened."[17] Perhaps not "simply," but the history of the expansion of Christianity is not an extension of the Acts of the Apostles, and Acts certainly does not provide a blueprint for church-wide evangelism programs. It is *post-apostolic* Christian growth that is most suggestive for the life of the church in our secular age

The Peculiarities of the Christian Society

The church lived and spoke the gospel in the particular context of the Roman Empire. The "glories" of Rome, evident in the remains of centuries-old structures and the pristine recreations of modern movies, should be viewed together with the underside of life in the totalizing imperial state: social dislocation, ethnic antagonisms, crushing poverty for the masses, urban disorder, and cultural chaos. All of this was accompanied by acute depopulation, frequent natural disasters, and plagues and other deadly epidemics. Roman life was marked by pervasive social distress that neither the empire nor its religions could alleviate.

17. Alan Kreider, *The Patient Ferment of the Early Church* (Grand Rapids: Baker Academic, 2016), 9.

Christians lived in the same circumstances, of course, but Christians responded to social dislocation and natural disaster in ways that set them apart. They lived distinctive lives shaped by cohesive communal convictions. The second-century apology, "Epistle to Diognetus," testified that "Christians cannot be distinguished from the rest of the human race by country or language or customs . . . Yet at the same time they give proof of the remarkable and admittedly extraordinary constitution of their own commonwealth."[18] Their unusual "commonwealth" was immediately evident in its composition. In the mid-second century, the Greek philosopher Celsus derided Christians for appealing to "illiterate and bucolic yokels, children, and stupid women." He was astonished that "they themselves admit that these people are worthy of their God."[19] The social inclusion of Christian communities incorporated a wide range of class, education, sex, and age. Especially notable was the mixing of slaves and masters, and the full inclusion of women, not only as members, but as leaders—patrons and *diakonoi*.

The unusual religious life of Christians was formed in closely knit communities, joined to sister communities across the empire in a new, universal family. Rodney Stark applies contemporary sociological categories to indicate the central difference between Christian and pagan cults: churches were "exclusive commitment organizations," pagan cults were "non-exclusive commitment organizations." Stark explains that nonexclusive religious organizations specialize in "*privately produced* religious goods," while exclusive religious organizations specialize in "the *collective production* of religion." When religious organizations function by providing *private* religious goods, they find themselves in competition with other providers of private goods, leading religious "consumers" to patronize multiple providers in order to satisfy their personal taste. Alternatively, when religious organizations exist to facilitate comprehensive *collective* goods, they require communal commitment that diminishes religious dabbling.[20]

Rather than seeking out one or many of the pagan cults to provide temporary personal benefit, persons were drawn to the church, which guided them in shaping a *shared life* distinguished by community practices

18. "Epistle to Diognetus," in Cyril C. Richardson, ed., *Early Christian Fathers*, (Philadelphia: Westminster, 1953), 216f.

19. Origen, *Contra Celcium* 3.44, translated by Henry Chadwick (Cambridge: Cambridge University Press, 1953), 153.

20. Rodney Stark, *The Rise of Christianity: A Sociologist Reconsiders History* (Princeton, NJ: Princeton University Press, 1996), 203ff.

centered in the One God, Father, Son, and Holy Spirit. Tertullian gives definition to "the peculiarities of the Christian society . . . We are a body knit
together as such to a common religious profession, by unity of discipline,
and by the bond of a common hope."[21] The church was ordered around
common faith, a unified way of life, and shared confidence, giving it a cohesion that contributed to its endurance in times of opposition and persecution, as well as its distinctive attractiveness in the midst of capricious "old
gods and new."

Christians responded to social stratification and dislocation, and to
natural disasters and disease, as a cohesive community that offered care,
not only to each other, but to pagans as well. Tertullian's *Apology* includes a
revealing description of the church's care for both Christians and pagans. In
explaining the nature of Christian associations and communal gatherings,
he contrasted the church's response to social misery to that of pagan cults.
How did the church live its faith in the use of its resources?

> There is no buying or selling of any sort in the things of God.
> Though we have our treasure-chest, it is not made up of purchase-
> money, as of a religion that has its price. On the monthly day, if he
> likes, each puts in a small donation, but only if it be his pleasure,
> and only if he be able: for all is voluntary. These gifts are, as it were,
> piety's deposit funds. For they are not taken thence and spent on
> feasts, and drinking-bouts, and eating-houses, but to support and
> bury poor people, to supply the wants of boys and girls destitute of
> means and parents, and of old persons confined now to the house;
> such, too, as have suffered shipwreck; and if there happen to be any
> in the mines, or banished to the islands, or shut up in the prisons,
> for nothing but their fidelity to the cause of God's Church, they
> become the nurslings of their confession. But it is mainly the deeds
> of love so noble that lead many to put a brand upon us, *See,* they
> say, *how they love one another.*[22]

Not just "one another," but also pagans in need. They provided food
and clothing for the poor, care for the sick, and burials for the indigent; they
opened their homes to orphans, including infants abandoned on trash heaps;
they cared for discarded slaves; they rescued sailors; and they provided for

21. Tertullian, "Apology," 39, in *Ante-Nicene Fathers*, vol. 3, translated by Sydney
Thelwall (New York: Scribner, 1905), 46.

22. Tertullian, "Apology," in *Ante-Nicene Fathers*, vol. 3, edited by Philip Schaff,
(Grand Rapids: Eerdmans, 1905), ch. xxxix, p. 46.

prisoners in Roman "gulags." All of these were "thrown-away people" in Roman society, thrown away by all except Christian communities.

The cohesive life of its communities also strengthened Christianity in its refusal to compromise with social customs and moral practices of the day. To be a Christian took far more than a sudden decision to believe; it took a radical change in the way one lived; it was not simply mental assent to God's truth, but living in God's Way. Christians condemned and would not tolerate in the church common practices of the day: infanticide, abortion, incest, polygamy, and divorce. Christianity taught and required honesty in commerce, fidelity in marriage, and steadfastness in charity. Christian faith and faithfulness was not easy adopt. Protracted catechetical instruction was required to induct converts into the demanding *habitus* of Christian life. They not only had a new narrative of God and humankind to learn, they had to embrace the new way the narrative required people to live. Many found it more difficult to live as Christians lived than to believe as Christians believed. The demands of initiation into the Christian community discouraged some, but attracted others who understood that they were embarking on a deeply meaningful journey together with others into a world-shattering way of life.

Although Justin, Tertullian, and others wrote *apologia*, appealing to the intelligentsia, the normal way of communicating the faith was through natural networks of family, friends, neighbors, and commercial contacts. There was no organized mission of the church, and no mass evangelism programs. Christians did not invite outsiders to "worship with us," and there is no evidence that individual Christians saw it as their duty to convert others to the faith. The faith was spread organically, through direct, intimate interpersonal association in existing social networks. "Above all," says Robin Fox, "we should give weight to the presence and influence of friends . . . One friend might bring another to the faith; a group of friends might exclude others and cause them to look elsewhere for esteem. When a person turned to God, he found others, 'new brethren,' who were sharing the same path."[23]

Christians were not made in a hurry. New birth meant entrance into a new *life*, and the church's catechesis aimed to shape new life before new Christians were invited to hear the gospel. In Alan Kreider's nice formulation, outsiders "said '*Vide*, look! How they love one another.' They did not

23. Robin Lane Fox, *Pagans and Christians* (San Francisco: Harper & Row, 1986), 316.

say, '*Aude*, listen to the Christians' message'; they did not say, '*Lege*, read what they write.' . . . Christianity's truth was visible; it was embodied and enacted by members."[24]

The Emerging Christian Minority

The difference between the church's first three centuries and the continuing effects of Constantinian establishment may be characterized by Kreider's formulation: "Conversion, which had made Christians into distinctive people—resident aliens—now was something that made people ordinary, not resident aliens but simply residents."[25] For most of its history, the church has resided as *the* religious reality of Europe and later of the Americas. For most of these centuries, Judaism was viewed as a continuing irritation, Islam as a periodic threat, and other world religions as exotica; Christianity was the taken-for-granted religious norm. All of that has ended now, although many in the church have not come to terms with the change; the church is now "the emerging Christian minority."

How does an emerging minority church proclaim the gospel in a secular age? Direct parallels with the church of the first three or four centuries are illusory, but certain realities press upon us. The church can no longer rely on a range of cultural props to sustain its tacit prominence in American consciousness. Cultural supports once made proclamation of the gospel easier, for it was possible to assume public familiarity with the Exodus, parables of the prodigal son and the good Samaritan, the Gospels' passion narrative, justification by faith, and other features of Christian faith. Cultural awareness made belief itself more natural, because the plausibility of faith's claims was woven into the social fabric. But in a secular, pluralistic age, when belief in the Christian gospel is "only one option among many," and an increasing number of persons "are just beyond it," the words we are accustomed to speaking find it difficult to gain a hearing.

Proclamation of the gospel in a secular age may find its initial grounding not in words, but in the character of the church's communal life—the *church's* life, not just the witness of exemplary Christians and exceptional congregations. The disciples of John the Baptist asked Jesus, "Are you the one who is to come, or shall we look for another?" Jesus responded, "Go

24. Kreider, *Patient Ferment*, 61.

25. Kreider, *The Change of Conversion and the Origin of Christendom* (Harrisburg, PA: Trinity International, 1999), 91.

and tell John what you have seen and heard." What there was to see and hear was remarkable: blind seeing, lame walking, the healing of lepers, deaf hearing, the dead living, and poor people hearing good news (Luke 7:18–23). What was visible was life different from the way things are. What does the church now have to say when people ask, "Are you the real thing, or shall we look elsewhere?"

Remember how Tertullian characterized the peculiarities of the Christian society: "We are a body knit together as such to a common religious profession, by unity of discipline, and by the bond of a common hope." Tertullian's words are not a mere sociological description, let alone a prescription for churchly success. They give voice to the fundamental qualities of a church that is capable of professing the gospel, because it is capable of living the gospel. Can we imagine an echo of Tertullian in a construal of the contemporary church in America as a *body knit together in common religious profession, unity of discipline*, and *common hope*?

A Body Knit Together

Tertullian's allusion to Ephesians 4:15–16 is obvious: "we are to grow up in every way into him who is the head, into Christ, from whom the whole body, joined and knit together by every joint with which it is supplied, when each part is working properly, makes bodily growth and upbuilds itself in love." The body is knit together *in* Christ, *by* Christ. The church is not a natural body, knit together by affinities of race, class, gender, age, or other shared features. Its "peculiarities" are found in its *un*natural composition. The astonishing inclusivity of the early church was itself a proclamation of the gospel, for it displayed a new life in Christ, where there was no longer distinction between Jew and Greek, slave and free, male and female, rich and poor, sick and well, learned and uneducated, young and old; no longer were there divisions among races and ethnicities. It was as the body birthed *by* Christ, the body *in* Christ, the body *of* Christ, that the church proclaimed Christ by displaying the birth of a new, communal way of life in and for the world.

Churches in contemporary America are not the church of the first three centuries. Too often, the churches exhibit the same tired partitions of race, class, ethnicity, and gender that are so apparent in the nation. The church has become a *typical* society, known by its conformity to prevailing social norms, not by its peculiarities. Some church growth gurus even advocate planned homogeneity as a prerequisite for effective outreach that will attract new members. The early church's inclusivity attracted new members, but this was not a growth strategy or an evangelism methodology. Ecclesial catholicity was a mark of the gospel, but it was not an independent characteristic of the early church. Rather than a *laissez-faire* assemblage, the "Christian society" was "knit together" in Christ by clear, nonnegotiable theological, organizational, and ethical norms.

Common Profession

The early church's *rule of faith* is a précis of its common religious profession. The rule of faith was not the imposed product of a centralized ecclesiastical authority, but an organic outgrowth of the need to teach the gospel to new Christians. Bishops throughout the church imparted central elements of the faith *after* it had been determined that catechumens were able to live as Christians lived. Hippolytus's *Apostolic Tradition* describes the ancient practice:

> And when they are chosen who are set apart to receive baptism let their life be examined, whether they lived piously while catechumens, whether they "honored the widows," whether they visited the sick, whether they have fulfilled every good work. If those who bring them bear witness to them that they have done thus, let them hear the gospel.[26]

New Christians were not ignorant of the church's faith, of course, for they worshiped with the community, listening to Scripture and its interpretation, but it was only at the climax of their incorporation into the body of Christ that they were taught and required to affirm the church's *common* religious profession as prerequisite for inclusion at the Lord's Table. Praxis preceded theological articulation, but theological articulation was necessary to knit the body together as a community of *faith*.

Churches in North America are characterized by the *absence* of common Christian profession. "Theological diversity" is their default conviction, hung on the scaffolding of tolerance, freedom of conscience, and bourgeois appropriations of apophatic theology. Churches may have clear confessional standards, but they are "symbols" in the ordinary rather than

26. Hippolytus, *The Apostolic Tradition*, edited by Gregory Dix & Henry Chadwick (London: Alban, 1937/1991).

the ecclesial sense. Catechesis in the churches is minimal, too often focused on denominational and congregational matters, and too seldom requiring deepened faith and amendment of life.

Unity of Discipline

The early church lived in patterns of mutual responsibility and account-ability. People were born again into a new *communal* life in which all were brothers and sisters in faith and in life. Their love for one another showed itself in frequent gatherings for worship, meals together, clothes closets and food pantries, praying for one another, welcoming travelers, caring for the sick and those in prison, solidarity with martyrs—in short, sharing new life in Christ. Their new life reached beyond the church, for loving care was given to all people, even to enemies, just as the Lord's love encompassed all. None of this was dependent on personal inclination, interest, or conve-nience; the *church* understood itself as obligated by the gospel.

Churches in contemporary America are "voluntary societies," in which many step forward not to serve, but to be served. This is not evi-dence of members' moral deficiency, for the churches advertise themselves as religious providers, catering to personal needs. Churches are not devoid of persons whose service within and beyond the community of faith is evi-dent in everything from taking flowers to shut-ins, teaching Sunday school, and sponsoring refugee families, to sheltering homeless people, building Habitat houses, installing water purification systems in Haiti, and working to combat racism in the church and society. But all of these are optional activities for those who are so inclined rather than the ecclesial norm. Loath to declare and cultivate common faith, and unwilling to describe and expect common life, the contemporary church's easy road to membership announces not the gospel, but the church's dispensability.

Common Hope

The early church's hope was placed in the mercy of God. Christians hoped in their own eternal salvation, yet shared hope was not limited to life be-yond death. The church was confident that God was working his purpose out in the world, for the world. Because the church knew that it would come to pass that the nations would flow to the mountain of the house of the Lord and that many peoples would learn God's Way and walk in his path (Isa 2:2–4), the church remained hopeful in the face of harassment, persecution, and martyrdom. Common hope in God and God's Way meant that the church did not have to plan its own future, devise its own strategies, create its own programs. The church was not passive, but rather confident, trusting in God, not presuming to control events.

Churches in America today are anxious, not hopeful. The prospect of institutional decline leads to a frantic succession of vision statements, strategic plans, measurable objectives, and the displacement of "outputs" by "outcomes," all dependent on the latest management trends. Hope in God's Way is replaced by reliance on the latest fads in management techniques accompanied by official expressions of optimism that sound eerily like whistles in the dark.

Call and Response

"When the church faces the prospect of its own demise," writes Michael Jinkins, "it faces a critical moment when its vocation is called into question, when it has unparalleled opportunity to comprehend and to render its life."[27] The church in America has not yet faced the prospect of its own demise, even though the trajectory of its decline is evident. If reality is faced, the church may find fresh angles of vision in openness to the life of our early ecclesial forebears and the life of our recent offspring. The early church and the church of the Global South may provide us with perspectives on our ecclesial life by removing the scales of *this* time and place from our eyes. But necessary awareness of the church's past and attention to the growing churches in the Global South are not sufficient to comprehend and render our ecclesial life. What is required is what has always been required: awareness of and attention to the call of the present Christ, who calls us to be one, to be holy, to be catholic, to be apostolic, to be the church.

27. Michael Jinkins, *The Church Faces Death: Ecclesiology in a Post-Modern Context* (New York: Oxford University Press, 1999), 13f.

6

Orthodoxy in America: A Minority That Came of Age

Anton C. Vrame

By ANY MEASURE, EASTERN Orthodox Christianity is a minority religion in the United States. It always has been and probably always will be. But there was never an attempt, from what I can determine, to actually count members and see how small of a minority it actually was. In the one hundred and fifty years since the Orthodox began establishing parishes in America—that is, when the immigrants began arriving on the East Coast from the Orthodox majority countries of the Balkans, Eastern Europe, and the Middle East—there were no systematic attempts to count the size of the population. Rhetoric, inflated rhetoric, was a sufficient tool to serve the community's needs.

It began early. At his enthronement address as Ecumenical Patriarch in 1921, Meletios IV (Metaxakis) famously noted, reflecting on his time in the United States (during which he organized the Greek Orthodox Archdiocese of North and South America), "the measure in which the name of Orthodoxy would be exalted . . . if the two million Orthodox Christians of America were organized into one united ecclesiastical organization."[1] If that number was accurate, the Orthodox population was 2 percent of the US population. A document of May 1955 read into the Congressional Record states that there were seven million Orthodox Christians in the United States.[2] If that number was accurate, then the Orthodox population had

1. C. Tarasar, ed. *Orthodox America: 1794–1976* (Syosset, NY: OCA, 1975), 189.

2. Statement of Sen. Estes Kefauver, Congressional Record, May 18, 1955. Archives of

grown considerably to nearly 5 percent of the US population. In a 1974 memo to President Ford preparing him for a visit from Archbishop Iakovos of North and South America to discuss the situation in Cyprus, the State Department informed the President that the Greek-American community had between two and a half and three million members.[3]

Today, the situation is more realistic, but not as satisfying as the rhetoric. Since 2000, there has been a more systematic counting of Orthodox Christians in the United States, mainly through the Faith Communities Today project.[4] There are not seven million Orthodox Christians in the United States; neither are there three million. According to the 2010 census of Orthodox Christians sponsored by the Assembly of Bishops in the United States, there are 797,500 adherents belonging to all the Byzantine Orthodox jurisdictions in the United States, with approximately 476,000 of them members of the Greek Orthodox Archdiocese of America.[5] The Pew Forum generously uses five tenths of one percent (0.5%) as the number of Orthodox in the US.[6]

As you might imagine, Orthodox Church leadership is uncomfortable with the reality of the census data. Leadership will often question the methods used to determine the number or just question the accuracy of the data outright, usually because they have witnessed a crowded parish somewhere. Greek Orthodox leadership has shifted its rhetoric, not offering a number, but saying things like, "The Greek Orthodox community is by far the largest Orthodox community in the United States." Most likely, this is due to the desire to be "greater" than we really are or to risk the loss of influence and access to civic authorities, especially the White House, which, as I hope to demonstrate in this paper, has been so successful for the community over the years. (Who in Washington, DC would pay attention to such a tiny group? Why would the leader of this tiny community be invited to offer a prayer at both Democratic and Republican Party conventions?)

the Greek Orthodox Archdiocese of America (hereafter Archives). I am especially thankful to Miss Nikie Calle, Archivist of the Greek Orthodox Archdiocese of America, for her assistance with the documents from the Archives pertaining to this paper.

3. President Ford's Meeting with Archbishop Iakovos, Oct. 4, 1974. Declassified memo. The Gerald Ford Library. Archives.

4. See Faithcommunitiestoday.org.

5. Alexei Krindatch, "Fast Questions and Fast Answers about US Orthodox Churches." www.orthodoxreality.org. Last accessed May 23, 2016.

6. Religious Landscape Survey, Pew Forum, May 2015.

My goal in this essay is to show that during the Second World War and in the 1950s, the Orthodox community ignored its minority status and used the rhetoric to its advantage, successfully achieving important goals for itself. First, it served its people by keeping clergy out of the draft and then having the religious affiliation of military personnel recognized. Second, the Church, by pursuing recognition as a "major faith," achieved a place in American social life that it had not claimed for itself before. In the process, the Orthodox claimed the "American story" as their own, as its members shifted their mentality to that of being an immigrant community to that of an American church. It also learned valuable lessons about how to operate in the American sociopolitical landscape, lessons it has used to this day while pursuing other interests. But, the story that I am sharing is the first time that the Orthodox Churches took these steps, and a result, I can call this period of time a "coming of age" story. The story that I want to share with you, apart from some broad brushstrokes, has not been looked at more carefully in decades, nor has the documentary evidence, contained in the archives of the Greek Orthodox Archdiocese, been brought to light.

Becoming a Major Religion

Seventy years ago, as World War II grew in intensity, the Orthodox Church communities in the United States first seemed to become aware that it had a problem with its status within American society. In 1942, Rev. John H. Gelsinger, a priest of the Syrian Orthodox Church (as the Antiochian Archdiocese of North America was called then), was not able to defer his military service under Class IV-D of the Selective Service Act of 1940. This classification was for clergymen and seminarians, making them ineligible for military service. But the Orthodox churches were not recognized as "regular churches" at the time under the act, thus "his status as a clergyman under the Selective Service Act was called into question."[7] The leadership of the Orthodox jurisdictions in the United States, bishops and lay, organized itself into the Federated Orthodox Greek Catholic Primary Jurisdictions in America (the first attempt at Orthodox administrative unity) and proceeded to make its case to the Army.

---

7. Concordat by the Orthodox hierarchs to the General Lewis Hershey, National Director, Selective Service System, 28 November 1942. Archives. See also George Papaioannou, *The Odyssey of Hellenism in America* (Thessaloniki: Patriarchal Institute for Patristic Studies, 1975), 480–81.

The case was made that, indeed, Fr. John was a priest of the one Eastern Orthodox Church. The case argued that the Eastern Orthodox churches, albeit divided jurisdictionally along ethnic lines, were a single Christian church, no matter whether their name was Syrian, Russian, or Greek. They argued:

> Orthodox Jurisdictions differ from one another only in language and nationality. Inasmuch as they are all of Greek rather than of Latin (Roman) tradition, the appellation *Greek* is properly common to them all. Inasmuch as they profess to preserve the unchanged and true (orthodox) doctrine of the Apostolic Age and of the Seven Oecumenical Councils, all of them are (and always have been) properly and officially known as *Orthodox*. Inasmuch as their historical continuity is the central theme and guiding clue in every treatise on the History of the Early Church, they are by universally accepted usage called *Catholic*. And inasmuch as their ritual, and—in some degree—their doctrinal outlook are characteristic of the Greek East in contradistinction to the ritual and doctrinal outlook of the Latin (Roman) West, they are community referred to as *Eastern*. Here there is ONE [sic] Orthodox Greek Catholic Church, and only one. This one Church is not divided into parts, because it is INDIVISIBLE (sic); but it is composed of many jurisdictions devised to suit the necessities of language and nationality. These Jurisdictions are often referred to as the *Eastern Orthodox Churches*.[8]

Thus, the memo argued, Fr. John and all Orthodox priests and seminarians should be treated as those of other denominations in the United States, that is, have his draft status classified under the provisions of IV-D status. The Federation concluded its argument with a statement, signed by the ruling hierarchs of the Orthodox jurisdictions in the United States at that time, to the Selective Service System:

> Therefore, both for the present case of the Rev. Fr. John H. Gelsinger and for the avoidance of similar confusion in other cases which may arise hereafter, the Orthodox Greek Catholic Hierarchs signatory hereto earnestly request that in the Selective Service Regulations a determination be noted which will apply to the whole Orthodox Greek Catholic Church, and therefore to all Orthodox Greek Catholic Clergy and to all Students who are being trained for the Orthodox Greek Catholic Priesthood.[9]

8. Concordat.
9. Concordat.

The determination requested "would safeguard the Orthodox Greek Catholic Church in the exercise of the American freedom of religion to which She is justly entitled, and which would leave Her unhampered in Her zealous striving to serve America in this time of war."[10]

The effort of the Federation was successful. On December 8, 1942, the Selective Service System recognized the Eastern Orthodox Church for the purposes of the act. In a memo addressed on December 9 to the Federation, Orthodox Clergy "have been exempt from military service and they are qualified to serve as Chaplains in the US Army."[11]

The Federation also pursued other avenues to secure recognition under the law as a legitimate ecclesiastical body in the United States. In 1943, in a historic first, the Assembly of the State of New York amended the Religious Corporations Law on March 25 so that it included the Orthodox Churches in the United States, thus officially recognizing the faith.

At some point, and the documentary record has a gap here, the Church apparently realized that in order to secure rights for its members and allow them to be served by chaplains, a greater effort at formal recognition was needed. While the initial effort with the Selective Service System was successful, Orthodox servicemen could not have "EO" or similar for "Eastern Orthodox" placed on their dog tags. The only possibilities were P for Protestant, C for Catholic, J for Jewish, or X for Other. Lobbying the Army directly to make this change in dog tags must have been unsuccessful because a new strategy appears to have been developed. But this effort would wait until after the War, in 1954.

The Greek Orthodox Church began a two-pronged approach.[12] First, Church leaders lobbied US Congressmen for an Act of Congress to permit the EO designation. Second, in an effort to secure "grassroots" support for the cause, state legislatures began to be lobbied to recognize the Orthodox Churches as a "major faith." This strategy is laid out clearly in a 1955 letter from Archbishop Michael to Mr. Paul Manolis, the Greek Orthodox Executive Secretary to Senator William Knowland of California. The Archbishop asked Manolis to "use his influence" with Senator Knowland to promote a bill to allow the EO designation. The Archbishop wrote:

10. Concordat.

11. Memo of George Phillies to His Eminence Archbishop Jacob (Iakovos Coucouzes), March 26, 1959. Archives.

12. The documentation for this effort is from Greek Orthodox sources: the Archdiocese, parishes, and individuals. The Federation no longer appears to be active during this effort.

s is to certify that the pen hereunto affixed was used by me in approving Senate Bill, Introductory Number 297, Print Number 794, by Mr. Burney, entitled:

"AN ACT to amend the religious corporations law, in relation
to the Federated Orthodox
Greek Catholic Primary Jurisdictions in America, and re-
numbering certain articles
thereof."

came a law March twentieth, being Chapter 145 of the Laws of 1943.

G I V E N under my hand and the
Privy Seal of the State at
the Capitol in the City of
Albany this twenty-second day
of March in the year of our
Lord one thousand nine hundred
and forty-three.

BY THE GOVERNOR:

Secretary to the Governor.

You no doubt know that our Church has for years been striving for official recognition by the Federal Government and that our Orthodox servicemen have always faced a problem in arranging to have the 'E.O.' designation affixed to their dog-tags. Thus far this Archdiocese has tried very hard to solve this dog-tag identification program, but we have met with little success. Recently we have tried for recognition through the State Senates. Five States, namely New York, Massachusetts, Wisconsin, Louisiana and West Virginia, have already passed similar laws recognizing officially our Church, and many others are expected to follow the example.[13]

The first attempt to have EO placed on dog tags by an Act of Congress came in 1954. Senator Leverett Saltonstall of Massachusetts had entered a bill. Unfortunately, as the correspondence shows, the bill was not taken up. In a September 9 letter, Archbishop Michael wrote to the Senator:

> As you have no doubt been informed the matter of designation of the Eastern Orthodox Faith on identification tags of the Armed Forces has been cause for concern not only for this Archdiocese but for all the Eastern Orthodox Churches in America. Your sponsorship and support of this bill (Senate Bill S.3872) is an action in keeping with the feeling of cooperation and understanding between the Churches and the political leaders of America. I am certain with your personal interest in this matter favorable action will ultimately result on this bill.[14]

Senator Saltonstall responded on October 7 to Archbishop Michael, writing: "Although the session did end before action was taken regarding the bill, I have of course kept in close touch with it. I was informed only last week that the Board of Chaplains of the Department of Defense is studying the bill and will make a report on it to the Senate Armed Service Committee, of which I am the Chairman."[15]

Continuing to be lobbied by Greek Americans, in the new session, in January 1955, Senator Saltonstall introduced a new bill, (S. 106) into the Senate record:

> Be it enacted by the Senate and House of Representatives of the United States of America in Congress assembled, that the Secretaries of the Army, the Navy, and the Air Force are directed to authorize the inclusion of the Eastern Orthodox religious faith as one of the religious faiths authorized to be designated as a religious preference on identification tags issued to members of the

13. Archbishop Michael to Paul Manolis, February 17, 1955. Archives.

14. Letter of Archbishop Michael to Senator Leverett Saltonstall, September 9, 1954. Archives.

15. Letter of Senator Leverett Saltonstall to Archbishop Michael, October 7, 1954. Archives.

Armed Forces. The capital letters "E.O." shall be used on such tags to indicate the designation of such faith.[16]

HOUSE CONCURRENT RESOLUTION NO. 37

A RESOLUTION RECOGNIZING THE EASTERN ORTHODOX CHURCH AS A MAJOR RELIGION IN THE STATE OF MISSISSIPPI, AND COMMENDING THEM FOR THE PROGRESS THEY HAVE MADE AND THE VALUE THEY REPRESENT TO ALL CITIZENS OF MISSISSIPPI.

WHEREAS, the Eastern Orthodox Church, along with other major faiths, represents a tremendous force for good in teaching our citizens respect for God and our Nation; and

WHEREAS, the Eastern Orthodox Church is considered a major faith in the United States and more than twenty-five of our sister states have now recognized this church as a major faith: NOW, THEREFORE,

BE IT RESOLVED BY THE HOUSE OF REPRESENTATIVES OF THE STATE OF MISSISSIPPI, THE SENATE CONCURRING THEREIN, That the Eastern Orthodox Church is recognized as a major faith in the State of Mississippi, and accorded the same rights, privileges, and respect that are accorded all other major religions.

ADOPTED BY THE HOUSE OF REPRESENTATIVES
March 26, 1964

SPEAKER OF THE HOUSE OF REPRESENTATIVES

ADOPTED BY THE SENATE
April 8, 1964

PRESIDENT OF THE SENATE

16. S. 106, 84th Congress, January 6, 1955. Archives.

The Department of Defense disagreed with the bill. In a letter from Robert Stevens, Secretary of the Army for the members of the Senate Armed Services Committee, of which Saltonstall was a member (along with such notables as Lyndon Johnson, Estes Kefauver, John Stennis, Henry Jackson, Sam Ervin, and Margaret Chase Smith), the argument put forward was:

> The designation of a general religious classification on identification tags is not for the purpose of giving recognition to any religious group but to facilitate giving proper ministrations in case of emergency. Furthermore, it is questionable whether a clergyman of one group could minister effectively to the members of all eighteen groups which are considered in the general classification of Protestants. For the above reasons, the Department of the Army on behalf of the Department of Defense recommends that S. 106 not be enacted.[17]

The Defense Department's objections to the bill became known and the grassroots campaign began. Peter Bell advised Archbishop Michael to contact prominent Greek Orthodox Americans in the States represented by the members of the Senate Armed Services Committee to lobby for passage of the bill.[18]

Bell's own letter went to Maxwell Rabb, a member of President Eisenhower's Cabinet. Rabb was an advocate for civil rights, so it was a well-placed letter. Bell's lengthy letter strongly challenged the Army's refusal, mentioned above. Bell writes to "Max" (it is unclear if they already knew one another):

> The logic . . . fails me. Perhaps you could persuade him or those in the Department under him who are making the decision to explain to us just how the "X" facilitates matters more than EO for Eastern Orthodox or let us say CS for Christian Science, or SDA for Seventh Day Adventist, or any such other designation. In any event, whatever the decision of the Department may be, it cannot be more important or of so overwhelming a nature that six million members of the Eastern Orthodox Faith in the United States have to be classified as second class religionists in the United States while the Protestant, Catholic and Jewish religions are recognized as first class religions.

A little later he continues in a rather harsh tone:

17. Robert Stevens to Senate Armed Services Committee. Archives.
18. Peter Bell to Archbishop Michael, April 1, 1955. Archives.

> Perhaps you could even ask some of those men in the Department
> of Defense to read a little American history. You might even per-
> suade them to read the Declaration of Independence and the Con-
> stitution of the United States which apparently, they have never
> taken the trouble to read or at least understand even though it is
> written in very plain language. I would not insult your intelligence
> by quoting from either of these great Documents concerning
> equality and the right to worship God according to the dictates of
> your conscience, and not according to the dictates of some bu-
> reaucrat in the Department of Defense.[19]

Senator Estes Kefauver, a member of the Armed Services Committee, placed a message in the Congressional Record on May 18, 1955 in support of Senate Bill 106. It is evident from his message that the Greek American community had reached him. In his message Kefauver states:

> Certainly the 7,000,000 Americans who are members of this faith
> merit this consideration. In past years members of this faith go-
> ing into the armed services, have to register either as a Protestant
> or Catholic, although the Greek Orthodox Church contends that
> neither designation properly applies. Young men of this faith have
> gladly laid down their lives in wars this nation has faught (sic).
> They are entitled to this small consideration.[20]

Kefauver's message includes a resolution from the Voice of Greek Orthodoxy in America. This resolution cites the origins of the Orthodox Church with Jesus Christ and his apostles, and the ancient patriarchates of Alexandria, Antioch, Jerusalem, and Constantinople. It notes that there are 250 million Orthodox Christians worldwide and 7,000,000 in the United States. It reminds the readers that Orthodox serviceman had to register as Catholics or Protestants indiscriminately. It points out the freedom of reli-gion and free exercise of religion clauses of the Constitution. It goes on to note how the Veterans Administration has allowed the Eastern Orthodox to conduct services and sacraments in VA hospitals. The final clauses point out that there are thousands of Orthodox servicemen and that thousands "have made the supreme sacrifice in fighting for the democracy of the world, one of which is the freedom of religion."[21]

19. Peter Bell to Maxwell Rabb, May 5, 1955. Archives.

20. Congressional Record, May 18, 1955. Archives.

21. Congressional Record, May 18, 1955. Archives

The Archdiocese grassroots campaign was directed to the men and women of the Greek Orthodox Youth of America (GOYA) organization, formally established in 1951. While today GOYA refers to high school-age students and youth ministry, in the 1950s it was a young adult ministry, comprised of many returning veterans and others from the "greatest generation."[22] It was reported that by 1958 there were 30,000 members of GOYA around the United States connected to most parishes of the Archdiocese.

Ann Hadjian, a GOYA leader in Canton, Ohio, relayed a message from Archbishop Michael to the GOYA chapters in Ohio, West Virginia, and Pennsylvania in May 1955:

> Archbishop Michael, in a telegram received today, requests that all Goyans be asked to send telegrams to their respective senators and representatives concerning Congressional Bill S-106 . . . Please take immediate action to notify all Goyans and Orthodox people in your community to wire their senators and representatives requesting their support of this Bill to bring about recognition of the Eastern Orthodox Church by the Armed Forces.

Attached to her letter was the text of the bill, the names of various Senators and Representatives, and five sample letters that could be sent to them.[23]

The second element of the strategy was for recognition of Eastern Orthodoxy by the States. As we saw from the 1955 memo to Manolis, it had the primary goal of putting pressure on the Federal Government to grant rights to Orthodox Church members in the military. This process initially began in 1943, picked up in 1953, and lasted into the 1970s, well after the EO designation was approved, but would prove to be useful with regard to other issues. The recognition could be pronounced in a resolution of a state assembly or in the form of legislation. The following examples are emblematic of the language used.

The State of Georgia used legislation in 1957. Its bill reads:

> Section 1. Where the names of major religious faiths, such as Protestants, Catholics and Jews, are used in resolutions, bills, acts, laws and other official papers of the State or any political subdivision thereof, the name of the Eastern (Greek) Orthodox Church shall

---

22. See Papaioannou, *Odyssey of Hellenism in America*, 174.
23. Ann Hadjian to GOYA Members of District 3, Diocese I, May 19, 1955

be included. Section 2. All laws and any parts of laws in conflict with this Act are hereby repealed.[24]

In 1964, the State of Mississippi used a Concurrent Resolution (No. 37) to state:

Be it resolved by the House of Representatives of the State of Mississippi, the Senate Concurring therein, that the Eastern Orthodox Church is recognized as a major faith in the state of Mississippi, and accorded the same rights, privileges and respect that are accorded all other major religions.[25]

24. State of Georgia, House Bill No. 370, March 5, 1957. Archives.

25. State of Mississippi, House Concurrent Resolution No. 37, March 26, 1964. Archives.

IN THE SENATE OF THE UNITED STATES

JANUARY 6, 1955

Mr. SALTONSTALL introduced the following bill; which was read twice and
referred to the Committee on Armed Services

84TH CONGRESS
1ST SESSION   **A BILL   S. 106**

To allow certain members of the Armed Forces to designate
the Eastern Orthodox faith as a religious preference on
their identification tags.

1   *Be it enacted by the Senate and House of Representa-*

2   *tives of the United States of America in Congress assembled,*

3   That the Secretaries of the Army, the Navy, and the Air

4   Force are directed to authorize the inclusion of the Eastern

5   Orthodox religious faith as one of the religious faiths au-

6   thorized to be designated as a religious preference on iden-

7   tification tags issued to members of the Armed Forces. The

8   capital letters "E. O." shall be used on such tags to indicate

9   the designation of such faith.

I

> In the United States today there are more than 5,000,000
> loyal American citizens of the Eastern Orthodox Church of whom many thou-
> sands serve their country faithfully in the Armed Services. However,
> though these thousands of Eastern Orthodox form a substantial part of the
> Armed Forces, they are not recognized on an equal basis with the other ma-
> jor religions.
> In order to rectify this inconsistency Senator Leverett
> Saltonstall of Massachussets has introduced the above bill in the United
> States Senate for the recognition of the Eastern Orthodox Faith in the
> Armed Forces.
> We request your support as an American citizen for the
> approval of this bill. We hope that you will send a letter to your Sen-
> ator supporting this bill, for such recognition is in keeping with the
> best American traditions.
>
>   A Public Service of the Greek Archdiocese

As 1980 began, forty-two states had recognized the Orthodox Church as a "major religion."[26]

The efforts of the Church were successful. The Defense Department reversed its earlier objections to the EO designation. On June 1, 1955,

26. They are: Alabama, Alaska, Arkansas, California, Connecticut, Delaware, Florida, Georgia, Idaho, Illinois, Indiana, Iowa, Kentucky, Louisiana, Maryland, Massachusetts, Michigan, Minnesota, Mississippi, Missouri, Montana, Nebraska, Nevada, New Hampshire, New Jersey, New Mexico, New York, North Carolina, North Dakota, Ohio, Oregon, Pennsylvania, Rhode Island, South Carolina, South Dakota, Tennessee, Texas, Virginia, Washington, West Virginia, Wisconsin, and Wyoming.

Archbishop Michael was able to send the following telegram to the leadership of the Orthodox jurisdictions in the United States:

> Am delighted to inform you the happy result of our recent combined efforts for the glory of our holy Eastern Orthodox Church. We are advised by Senator Saltonstall and Congressman Dorn that the Defense Department has approved the placing of E.O. on dog tags. No legislation now required. This has undoubtedly been made possible only through our close cooperation. This memorable success leads the way to continued cooperation for the benefit of all Eastern Orthodox Communicants in America.[27]

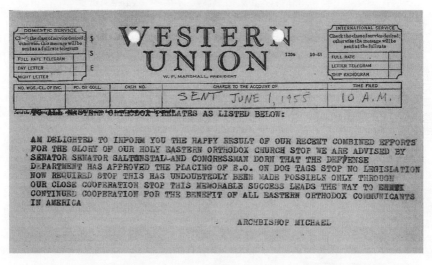

A similar congratulatory telegram was sent to lay people, Goyans, and others around the United States, including: Spyros Skouras (20th Century Fox, NY), Stephen Skopas (President of AHEPA), Peter Chumbris, Andrew Vance (Washington, DC), Paul Manolis (Washington, DC), Tom Pappas (Boston), John Legelis (NYC), Charles Paterson (Worcester, MA), Ann Hadjian (Canton, OH), Peter Bell (Worcester), Anthony Elafopoulos (NYC), and George Petite (Baltimore, MD). This list points to the efforts of the Archdiocese to persuade important personalities in the community, especially those with the ability to reach members of Congress, to use their influence to secure the desired outcome. The Archbishop also sent

27. Archbishop Michael Western Union telegram, June 1, 1955 to Abp Anastasius, Dr. G. Florovsky, Rev. B. HAtegan, Bp. Bohdan, Abp. Samuel David, Bp. Dionysius, Met. Leonty, Bp. Markos, Bp. Orestes. Archives.

congratulatory and thankful messages to Senator Saltonstall (R-MA), Representatives Francis Dorn (R-NY) and George Huddleston (D-AL).

While this story seems to have a happy ending, naturally the reality is more complicated. While the Defense Department did reverse its objection to the EO designation, it did not begin a process of calling in already issued dog tags to issue new tags with the EO. Whatever the serviceman had on them was going to stay unless the serviceman requested new tags with the EO designation. New and future servicemen would be allowed to place EO on their dog tags.[28]

An Epilogue

The Archdiocese made one final push for recognition in the United States Congress. House Resolution 888 was entered on June 14, 1966. It resolved,

> Whereas it follows that a religious distinction is being made in omitting the Eastern Orthodox Church, which is contrary to the prevailing principle of democracy and freedom of religion in this country: Now, therefore, be it resolved, that the Eastern Orthodox Church is a major faith in this country; and that all references by Federal agencies to major faiths now limited to Protestants, Catholics, and Jews include the Eastern Orthodox Church.

28. Paul Manolis to Archbishop Michael, August 3, 1955. Archives.

89TH CONGRESS
2D SESSION

H. RES. 888

IN THE HOUSE OF REPRESENTATIVES

JUNE 14, 1966

Mr. CULVER submitted the following resolution; which was referred to the Committee on the Judiciary

RESOLUTION

Whereas the Eastern Orthodox Church is a major faith in the United States and throughout the world; and

Whereas Senate bill 106, Eighty-fourth Congress, led to the designation of the Eastern Orthodox faith as a separate religious faith in the Armed Forces of the United States; and

Whereas several Federal agencies have omitted Eastern Orthodoxy in projects in which Protestant, Catholic, and Jewish faiths have been invited to participate; and

Whereas more than half of the States in the United States through their legislators have passed resolutions recognizing Eastern Orthodoxy as a major religious faith; and

Whereas the Eastern Orthodox faith has millions of communicants throughout the world including several million in the United States; and

.V.

The resolution noted that Senate Bill 106 recognized Eastern Orthodoxy as a separate faith in the Armed Forces, even though passage of the bill was never obtained nor required once the Defense Department changed its mind. The House Resolution notes that "more than half of the States in the United States . . . have passed resolutions recognizing Eastern Orthodox as a major religious faith; and . . . the Eastern Orthodox faith has millions of communicants throughout the world including several million in the United States."[29]

2

Whereas where anything is said concerning the major faiths, usually the Protestant, Catholic, and Jewish faiths are referred to; and

Whereas it therefore follows that a religious distinction is being made in omitting the Eastern Orthodox Church, which is contrary to the prevailing principle of democracy and freedom of religion in this country: Now, therefore, be it

1   *Resolved*, That the Eastern Orthodox Church is a major
2 faith in this country; and that all references by Federal
3 agencies to major faiths now limited to Protestants, Cath-
4 olics, and Jews include the Eastern Orthodox Church.

This resolution was referred to the Senate Judiciary Committee. Unfortunately, Senator Everett Dirksen (R-IL) wrote to the Greek Orthodox Archdiocese that the bill would probably not come out of committee because members felt that the Supreme Court decisions barring prayer in the public schools made passing the bill impossible. However, Dirksen still encouraged the members of the Church to write to their Congressmen and Senators and pursue recognition through other means, such as testifying at Congressional hearings on issues, such as immigration, where Roman Catholic, Protestant, and Jewish clergy also testified.[30]

Dirksen's advice must have been taken. In 1980, the Archdiocese was gratified to announce that, "in the December 1979 Bulletin of the United States Army's Regulations (AR 165–20) for the first time the Orthodox Church is included." In the news release, Archbishop Iakovos stated that

29. House Resolution 888, 89th Congress, 2nd Session (June 14, 1966). Archives.

30. "Orthodoxy Gains as a Major Faith in United States But Recognition by Congress Unlikely Says Senator Dirksen," News Release, Greek Orthodox Archdiocese of America, July 1966. Archives.

this action "has great significance, because it acknowledges that the Orthodox Church is in fact the Fourth Major Faith in our country."[31]

Lessons Learned

There are plenty of lessons from this story, but the following stand out, and demonstrate how this moment in time was a "coming of age" story for the Orthodox in America.

First, we see the Church learned from this strategy and its experience. As mentioned earlier, the Church continued to press for recognition as a major faith. It would use this status to request a seat at the table on subsequent issues that were important to it. The Church used this status for access to the White House and Capitol Hill to advance its interests after the July 1974 Turkish invasion of Cyprus and the simultaneous fall of the military dictatorship in Greece, including support for the new democratic government in Greece, the status of the Greek-Cypriot refugees from the occupied part of the island, an arms embargo on Turkey, and the maintenance of the 7:10 ratio of arms sales from the United States to Greece and Turkey. By this time though, the Church was also actively using the grassroots approach of lobbying members of Congress and taking advantage of church members now being elected to Congress. Personally, I recall being encouraged by Church leaders to write Senators and Representatives about these matters.

More recently, over the last decade, we have seen the Order of St. Andrew, the Archons of the Ecumenical Patriarchate, use this same approach of personal connection, lobbying states while also pursuing the same agenda in Washington, to push for greater freedom of operation for the Patriarchate in Istanbul (Constantinople). The Religious Freedom Resolutions project was launched in 2006 to persuade every state in the United States to adopt a resolution in support of the Ecumenical Patriarchate. So far, forty-four state legislatures have done so.[32] Simultaneously, the Order has made similar appeals in Congress and to the White House. This time, they have been able over the years not to go to staff members, but to Greek Orthodox Senators, such as Paul Sarbanes (Maryland) and Olympia Snowe (Maine) and Representatives, such as Gus Bilirakis (Florida).

---

31. "Orthodox Church Included in US Army Regulations for the First Time," News Release. Greek Orthodox Archdiocese of America, January 19, 1980. Archives.

32. See http://www.archons.org/resolutions. Last accessed May 30, 2016.

As a last recent example, the Archdiocese of America used its rela-
tionships in New York to persuade Governor Andrew Cuomo to break the
impasse between the Archdiocese and the Port Authority of New York so
that the St. Nicholas Shrine could be relocated and built at "Ground Zero."
As you might recall, St. Nicholas Greek Orthodox Church, located in the
shadow of the World Trade Center, was demolished in the collapse of the
South Tower on September 11.[33] The Archdiocese had taken the Port Authority to court in an attempt to obtain a proper site to rebuild the church.
The Archdiocese, using its many personal contacts in the State Assembly
of New York and to Governor Cuomo, was able to persuade the Governor
to break the impasse and grant a permit for the site at 130 Liberty Street,
facing the 9/11 Memorial. The church, designed by Santiago Calatrava, is
under construction, but no opening date has been announced as of June
2018.

33. "St. Nicholas Issue Resolved, Church to Be Rebuilt!" *Orthodox Observer* 76 (October 2011) 1.

Throughout this lobbying work, the Church never seemed to forget that its mission is to minister to its people. The continual theme of the discussions and arguments with the military during the 1940s and 1950s was the concern that the Church had for its members, in this example, the members of the military. Church leaders wanted their members' religious identity to be recognized in order that they be ministered to appropriately, certainly in the case of an emergency (meaning life-threatening), but in other ways as well. Orthodox clergy would begin to serve as chaplains in the military and offer services to Orthodox Christians and others, as all chaplains do.

Third, the Church was indifferent to its minority status. While we might smile at the inflated and inconsistent numbers being used by the Orthodox to justify their claims for privileges, I suggest that the Orthodox leaders at the time were basically indifferent to their status as a minority group in the United States. Claiming to be a "major religion," and later the "fourth major religion" in the United States, had little to do with numbers in the United States, and far more to do with the claims of Orthodox Christianity as a religious faith tracing itself back to Christ and the apostles, with hundreds of millions of adherents in the world. This was the act of a community that was recognizing its place in the religious world, with a distinct identity from other Christian communities and especially the hegemonic Protestant and Roman Catholic communities of the United States. These claims far outweighed any numerical argument.

Fourth, the community was not afraid to use its connections with people of influence. Researching this presentation in the archives, reading the handful of letters between church leaders and significant senators and representatives, such as Saltonstall, Kefauver, Dorn, and Knowland, is pretty amazing. But once you get past being starstruck, we also see the Church not being afraid to speak to the highest levels of power at the time. It is speaking up for itself in a manner that had not seen in the earlier years of its life in America. The Church had matured enough and had begun to be known in such cities as Boston and New York so that it could, quite comfortably, press its case directly to senators and representatives. Of course, this may have also been part of the reason that Archbishop Michael would deliver a prayer at the second inauguration of President Eisenhower in 1957, the first time an Orthodox hierarch would offer such a prayer.

Relatedly, members of the community had become power brokers in their own right and the Church reached out to them for assistance. Saltonstall referred to Charles Patterson of Boston, a member of the Archdiocese, as a "young legislator."[34] As a second and more prominent example, we can see Spyros Skouras, the President of 20th Century Fox during those years, as someone the Church could turn to help it in its causes. While there is no evidence in the archives that Skouras was directly involved, that the Church included him in the telegram sharing the news that they had won their argument with the Army at least suggests that he was being kept in the loop on the issue.

Finally, in the many appeals for recognition, we hear the voices of Orthodox Americans claiming the American story for itself. The actors in this story are largely the children and grandchildren of immigrants. They saw themselves as Americans, wanting the rights and privileges of freedom of religious expression and identity that all other Americans had. That they had served in the Armed Forces during the Second World War was evidence of their loyalty to American ideals and service to the country. (A decade or so later, in the 1960s, we would see many of the same Orthodox Americans join Archbishop Iakovos in the Civil Rights movement work to extend these same rights and privileges to the Black community in the United States.) They stated the principles of American democracy and claimed them for themselves, demonstrating that they were moving beyond their immigrant community status and had come of age as an American church.

34. See Saltonstall to Archbishop.